# Reading and the Individual

HELEN HUUS
University of Missouri

THIS PRESENTATION focuses on the individual and how reading affects him. The implications, however, are like dropping a pebble. into the pond—the ever widening ripples spread in all directions.

It is not my purpose here to delineate the methods for teaching individuals how to read, nor to show how a teacher can cope with individual differences in a class. The purpose here is to analyze the interaction between the individual and his reading and to recognize the contribution reading can make to his total development. Four points will be discussed.

First is *purpose*. Reading for what? To what end? Is reading necessary in an electronic age where nonprinted means of communication abound? Ong (6) points out that communication leading to technological culture has passed through three stages: 1) where all verbal communication was oral, 2) where verbal communication was put into writing and reached its fullest development with the invention of movable alphabetic type, and 3) where verbal communication was reduced to code with the invention of the telegraph and was refined in the modern electric computer. Other electronic devices, like television, have brought sight and sound into new prominence.

Oral cultures had no way to preserve their records, except through bards, storytellers, or others who remembered events. With the advent of writing, individuals who wished to learn could do so independently and objectively. The electronic age has given a new organization to communication; but, as Ong points out, this, too, has been built upon the accumulated experience with oral and printed forms. People did not stop talking when printing was invented; neither will people stop reading because computers and

1

television have been invented. What is different now is the effect on individuals who can be in constant touch with global and space events as they occur—not hours or days later. To understand, assimilate, and put into perspective the information and attitudes presented through these avenues requires a background the individual can probably best receive through print. So, too, will the technicians, punch-card operators, office staffs, programers, directors, and inventors be dependent upon printed records and sources to accomplish their work. Input into computers is still dependent upon reading; and one of the products of the computer is the printout, which must be read. Even when computers become sophisticated enough to process the human voice, store it, and use it as output, the printed word—and reading—will still be needed, if for nothing more than the catalog; for there will still be those who wish to compare, retrace, and be stimulated by the printed page.

Nor should the aesthetic value of seeing, holding, and reading a beautiful book be minimized. If individuals develop standards for their own taste, they need to have experience with books de-designed and illustrated with artistry and good taste, not a sterile, square-box computer or pulpy paperbacks.

Granted that reading is likely to be available in the future, to what end shall an individual read? Not long ago a third grade class was asked by its teacher (1) to answer the question "Why Should I Learn to Read?" Some of the answers are enlightening:

> There are many reasons why I should read. I must be a good reader to study all my subjects at school, such as math, social studies, English literature, and science. I must be a good reader to read instructions on how to do things. I want to be a good reader so I can enjoy reading magazines and good books for pleasure.
>
> If I didn't know how to read, I couldn't read the newspapers, help my children with their school work, and when I drive (when I'm older) I couldn't read traffic and highway signs. You will not be able to go to parties because you would not know how to read the invitations.
>
> You should learn to read because when you grow up you will not know what is going on if you cannot read the news-

paper and magazines. We read because we need to know if it is the right thing, but if we do not know how to read, we would not understand other people. Also it is fun to read.

When you want to get a job, you will not get one because you do not know how to read, and they will say you should have learned to read. You will try and try, but you will not get a job. So learn to read.

The children saw the functional, social, vocational, and recreational aspects of reading, both for the present and the future. If they were typical children, they also spent about twenty hours a week looking at television, but still saw the purposes for learning to read.

Teachers need to help pupils realize the need for reading in terms of their own aspirations and desires.

Second is the individual's *acceptance of responsibility* for his own learning. Often pupils come from homes where they are cared for by adults who love them and give them support and encouragement. Even in homes where children are neglected, much may not have been demanded of them, though of course just *being* neglected demands a great deal of children. All these children come to school; and whether it is in the first grade where they are expected to learn to read or whether it is in any grade above the first, many refuse to face the task and try to evade it in any possible way. Younger pupils sometimes get a stomachache; older ones get a headache. Some of the pupils attempt to preserve their self-images by not trying to learn, for thus they have not failed. *If* they had tried, they console themselves, they could have learned. Some do not try and so do not learn.

Others try, reluctantly, but need the continued support and encouragement of teachers and parents every step of the way. There are still others who approach each new problem with confidence, anticipation, and evident enjoyment. There are more of the latter than a teacher may recognize in the preoccupation with others who need much help. They should not be forgotten because they, too, are individuals! Various types of learners are found at every level of education, but sensitive teachers will do their best to give the support and encouragement plus the instructional help that should result in learning.

Students must assume the responsibility for consciously concentrating, listening, applying, and remembering what they are trying to learn. Regardless of how long it takes a teacher to prepare a lesson, how carefully she has sequenced the learning steps to fit an individual, or how adroitly she presents the materials and ideas in a lesson, no teacher can learn for the student. Although the student may have to discipline himself when class gets dull or the teacher a little less scintillating than the television programs he would like to see, he must do *his* learning for himself.

The acceptance of learning for oneself adds another dimension to accountability, a term which is bandied about in educational circles today. Accountability is not new, for responsible people have always been accountable when asked. Teachers who are doing their jobs well have nothing to fear; in fact, they should welcome this public visibility. If school administrators *could* do better with their time, staff, facilities, and pupils, perhaps the fact of an accounting will give them the needed motivation to do the best they can.

However, when comparisons are made, it is important that comparable aspects be evaluated—that factors such as time spent, kind of materials available, pupil-teacher ratio, salary level, quality of students, and direct and concomitant learnings be considered—not just scores on standardized tests.

Success in mastering something new contributes to the development of the individual's self-concept. Does he see himself as achieving, or does he see himself as constantly failing? Many students are defeated before they start and because of their attitude they do fail. They do not put forth the effort they could. Certainly school is one place where all children should have an even chance. What they do with it is their responsibility. The small increments of success which they see serve as motivations for still other small increments, until the students become convinced that they *can* learn.

Since resiliency and perseverance are characteristics of achievers, some underachievers need to cultivate these traits to succeed. Teachers must help students recognize the small increments of growth in reading and other subjects that will provide the motivation for continued study so that pupils can independently ferret out what they need and want to know from the printed page. To make the pupils independent is a major instructional aim, though some teachers, like mothers, hesitate to "let go."

Third is the development of the *thinking* individual. This point emphasizes that man is a rational animal, but it also recognizes his right to be different. Booth (2) points out that "the man who cannot think for himself, going beyond what other men have learned or thought, is still enslaved to other men's ideas." Too often in our society, the man on the street waits to see what the popular trend will be before he pledges his thoughts, money, or efforts to a cause or an idea. If a democratic society is to remain truly democratic, each individual must do his own thinking and not be swayed by the last person he heard, read, or saw. If what Hutchins (5) says is true, that "the use of television in the United States in the 1960s can be put in its proper light by supposing that Gutenberg's great invention had been directed almost entirely to the publication of comic books," not much thinking is likely to result from being glued to the video screen.

Independence of thought must be based upon a background of information (much of which can be acquired only by reading); upon the ability to sift and weigh data; upon the ability to judge relevance and internal consistency; and upon the ability to accept, evaluate, and integrate new data when they appear. Booth (2) recognizes the role that critical thinking assumes, for he identifies as the most important mark of a truly educated man "the habitual effort to ask the right critical questions and to apply rigorous tests to our hunches."

Beyond the educated man, however, is the society of which he is a part. Will he analyze the many problems of his day: overpopulation, poverty, war, and pestilence; the fate of public education in America; the economic and educational needs in underdeveloped countries; and the making of a healthful, beautiful environment for all to enjoy in their leisure time? Will the individual analyze or will he blindly follow, caught up in mob psychology, and go his way complaining? Or will he, through constructive channels, try to alleviate some of the difficulties in his own area? The problems remain the same, but the attitude of optimism or pessimism can make a difference. Perhaps it is time to do a turnabout and move forward optimistically rather than wallow longer in self-pity and pessimism. An attitude of optimism is more in keeping with the American tradition than a defeatist attitude. According to Gardner (3), "Andre Maurois once said of Americans, 'In a word, they are optimists,' and the judgment still holds good. . . . The capacity of our people to believe stubbornly and irrepressibly that this is a world worth saving, and that intelligence and energy and good will might save it, is one of the most endearing and bracing of American traits."

Nor does this mean that there is only one way to achieve progress or self-fulfillment. Diversity has always been possible in an open-ended society, and Western civilization from Aristotle to the Renaissance man to Margaret Mead has been built upon the contributions of diverse elements in the society. Platt (7), a professor of physics, maintains that

> . . . Progress would be faster and life more interesting if we pursued more diverse goals—goals of excellence to be sure, but goals of our own, different from what everybody else is pursuing—and if we tolerated and encouraged the same sort of individuality in others. I want life to be various. I want to see around me not only apple trees but pear trees, not only fruit trees but slow-growing oaks and evergreen pines and rosebushes and bitter but salubrious herbs and casual dandelions and good old spread-out grass. Let us be different, and enjoy the differences.

Educators have long been aware of individual differences. Recently the term "divergent thinking" has come into the educational vocabulary. Research by Getzels and Jackson points out that there are aspects of creativity (or diversity) which bear little relation to intelligence as formerly measured (7). What is the individual's goal in life for himself and his children in this society? Should not individuals have the chance to develop skills they do not possess, to develop different ways of solving their problems, to do something badly, perhaps? Do the goals of education, as education for living in a society, need redefining? Are individuals learning how to conserve their health; to live in clean, comfortable, attractive homes and cities; to utilize their mental power to achieve satisfaction from *knowing* in addition to *using;* to live in harmony with their fellow men—at least to live and let live? These are the important questions to ask and to answer.

Teachers need to see in their day-to-day lessons—those that accumulate, 180 days a year, twelve or thirteen years, to high school graduation—the building blocks toward these larger goals. Little children—and older ones, too—can start by picking paper off the floor, not writing on walls, and not throwing candy wrappers on the playground. The larger goals can be accomplished only if a start is made.

Fourth is the necessity for *self-renewal* as a lifelong pursuit. The learning individual is curious, open-minded, and thoughtful. He can accept new ways of doing and thinking. To be a perpetual learner requires an objective view of self, as Socrates knew so well; enough self-confidence and courage to be willing to fail (or at least to look foolish in the pursuit); motivation from within rather than from external sources; and enough energy, drive, and enthusiasm to see the project through, even when the going becomes difficult. Individuals who have accepted the responsibility for their own learning, who have learned to think critically, and who have learned to function independently and creatively, must take the last step and commit themselves to a larger goal beyond themselves. Unless they do, individuals themselves may survive, but society will collapse.

Pioneers in any field—whether it be exploration, mountain climbing, botany, women's rights, or space—exemplify the self-renewing characteristics. Without the confidence, perseverance, and commitment to an ideal, these pioneers would never have succeeded. Societies have become solidified and structured with customs and traditions that hinder self-renewal. The basic problem in many societies today, including our own, is not the development of technology but the development of an organization that makes adequate provision for human beings to use the technology to find meaningful lives. Then the individual will know who he is, from whence he came, and where he is headed.

But the answer may be disappointing for the person who believes that once his physical needs are met—when he finally lives in the comfort and style to which he aspires—the answer has been found. Already the affluent society has given at least a segment of the society the material comforts it demands. That society, then, should be supremely happy. But does the answer lie in the acquisition of *things?* It may not be too long before all segments of society will have the physical comforts they need and wish. What then? How will leisure time be used? Is a perpetual beach-boat-recreation-animal kind of existence enough? History has shown that a society dies when the ideal for which it was originated has been achieved or when some vigorous, energetic group, committed to an ideal of its own, overruns the apathetic populace.

The only prevention lies in the possibility of continual self-renewal, not only of individuals but also of the society. As individuals who are members of the society continue to renew themselves, so has the society a chance to renew itself. Self-renewal is needed not only in body but also in mind and spirit. Evidences of self-renewal are seen already in the back-to-school movement of housewives whose children are at last in school; in the increasing night school attendance of young employees; and in the large number of informal groups within neighborhoods, clubs, and private agencies that entice adults to continue their learning. Some need to learn how to do a second or third job, for theirs have disappeared in the wave of automation. For many others, this new interest in learning has no vocational aim at all; it is merely a means of self-renewal that brings a satisfaction not achievable in any other way.

Teachers of reading have a fundamental role to play in helping the individual—and ultimately the society—to gain the skills that will enable him to launch out in many diverse directions, as he pursues the self-renewal that gives his life meaning and makes it all worthwhile. Such a teacher is described by Heisenberg (4) who states:

> Classroom lessons generally allow the different landscapes of the world of the mind to pass by our eyes without quite letting us become at home in them. According to the teacher's abilities they illuminate these landscapes more or less brightly and we remember the pictures for a shorter or a longer time. However, very occasionally, an object that has thus come into our field

of view will suddenly begin to shine in its own light—first, dimly and vaguely, then ever more brightly, until finally it will glow through our entire mind, spill over to other subjects, and eventually become an important part of our own life.

Such brightness the teachers of reading can help achieve.

## REFERENCES AND NOTES

1. Bailey, Barbara. Teacher of third grade, Boone School, Kansas City, Missouri.
2. Booth, Wayne C. (Ed.). *The Knowledge Most Worth Having*. Chicago: University of Chicago Press, 1967.
3. Gardner, John W. *Self-Renewal: The Individual and the Innovative Society*. New York: Harper and Row, 1963.
4. Heisenberg, Werner: "A Scientist's Case for the Classics," *Harper's Magazine*, May 1958, 25-29.
5. Hutchins, Robert M. *The Learning Society*. New York: New American Library, 1969.
6. Ong, Walter J. "Media and Culture," *University of Chicago Magazine* (March/April 1969), 25-27.
7. Platt, John R. "Diversity," in Wayne C. Booth (Ed.), *The Knowledge Most Worth Having*. Chicago: University of Chicago Press, 1967, 109-140.

# Phasing Reading Development: A Plea

JOHN T. THORNTON, JR.
Stephen F. Austin State University

WE HAVE BEEN CHALLENGED to eliminate the serious reading difficulties experienced by one out of every four students and to obtain universal literacy throughout the nation by the end of the 1970s (1). It has become increasingly apparent that the schools of the seventies will be held accountable for performance. In the sixties teachers placed demands upon society to better their lot, and rightly so. Now in the seventies society is demanding results. If there is doubt of this demand, one has only to read a current magazine (11). Edinger and Sands (6) point out that ". . . the old era of blind, unquestionable faith in schools is over." The time will soon end when parents can be satisfied by a teacher's explaining what is being done with a whole class instead of telling specifically how each child is being helped. This demand for performance will not be limited to parents, nor will it be only on the elementary and secondary level. It will also be felt on the college campus. The foregoing is not to imply that the schools have failed. In fact, as Gates (8) and Cremin (4) report, there is mounting evidence to the contrary. Children are reading better today than their predecessors of 25 years ago. Progress has been made with some children; but the fact remains that in spite of the fine efforts, there are children who are not being reached.

Any discussion of improving reading instruction involves the question of which method or approach works best. There has yet to be found the one method that teaches all children equally well. In an effort to reach all children with a single approach teachers may lose sight of the individual and the necessity of adapting instruction to the specific needs of each child. Educators have long talked about individual differences but in actual practice have been reluctant to accept these differences in the classroom. Educators have tried to group children so that differences would not exist and have searched for a method that would encompass all the differences.

10

Such practices, according to Gans (7), have led to a belief that one set of materials and specified methods will teach all children to read. This practice has resulted in teachers' being less inclined to meet individual differences, overdependence on how-to-do instructions, lack of creative teaching, less time for personally selected reading, limited sharing of stories and class discussion, and more commercially prepared work. The foregoing should not be the case. The results from the beginning reading studies sponsored by the U.S. Office of Education indicate that teachers, not methods, account for the major differences in the results of the studies and that reading instruction can be improved by combining methods.

For too long educators have been program oriented, thinking that what is good for one child must be good for all. It is time that a teacher be permitted to select the materials and methods that work best with the children for whom she is responsible. Along with the emphasis on the "right-to-read," an emphasis on the "right-to-teach" is needed.

## Basic Considerations

The following considerations seem to be necessary if teachers are to phase reading instruction with the child's overall development.

*Total child growth.* Reading is an integral part of total child growth. Reading is dependent upon growth in other areas, and it affects other growth areas. The literature abounds with studies which show the relationship between physical, mental, emotional, and social maturity and performance in reading. As teachers, do we also consider that reading performance affects other areas of development?

A positive self-image is one of the most important parts of early learning. It is important that the manner in which we teach reading does not cause children to feel defeated and unsure of themselves. It is the wise teacher that will not allow a child who is not ready for independent effort to be placed in a situation where he will become discouraged.

*Each child unique.* An examination of child development calls attention to the uniqueness of the individual and the importance of providing an environment which allows children to grow and mature at their own rates of development. Any discussion of individual differences would be incomplete without considering reading readiness. MacGinitie (*12*) explains the concept of readiness by asking the question, "The child is in school to learn—what and how is he ready to learn?" This question places readiness in proper perspective. It is not an all-or-nothing situation. Readiness encompasses the whole idea of phasing reading development with child development. It depends on the method and materials that are used and on the level at which instruction begins.

Dechant (*5*) points out that to know a child a teacher must be aware of the pupil's preferred mode of learning. Some children learn more easily through an auditory approach; others prefer a visual approach; and still others rely upon an kinesthetic approach. Realizing that children do differ in their sensory approaches to learning, the teacher has the responsibility of identifying the child's preferred mode of learning before selecting a method to use with him.

In keeping with the idea of how the child learns, much has been said about children discovering new ideas or new relationships for themselves. Almy (*2*) has suggested that this is the essence of Piaget's theory. New ideas are acquired by the child's trying them out within the context of his previous learning. To accomplish this goal a child needs opportunities to question, share ideas, react to situations, and test or try out his ideas on others. In selecting materials it should be kept in mind that programed materials do not provide these types of experiences. This statement is not to imply that programed materials are not of value in the teaching of reading. A better balance, however, is needed in the types of activities engaged in during the school day. Too much of the day in too many schools is spent by students "quietly working at their desks." What makes this activity really sad is that it is often thought of as individualized instruction.

Harris (*9*) suggests that individual differences in interest patterns are more important than differences in age, sex, intelligence, or reading achievement. The importance of interest can best be illustrated by the example of a fifth grade boy named Ricky. He was showing little progress in reading despite the combined efforts of several specialists and much individual help in the classroom. One day Ricky told his teacher he would like to be a boy scout and asked if the teacher would help him. Using the *Boy Scout Manual,* Ricky made more progress in reading than had ever been imagined possible by those working with him. If we are to develop lifelong readers, we must do more than just provide materials which match the child's interests. Our major concern should be to help children develop broader and more advanced reading tastes. This goal can more readily be accomplished by providing children with a wide variety of reading experiences. Beery (3) writes:

> We should reappraise any program that suggests that children should spend more time in talking or studying about reading than in reading.

The nation will be watching during the seventies! The challenge is before us to see that all children are provided the "right to read." If we fail to adapt instruction to the developmental needs of children, then we will have to live with the terrible thought expressed by the judge in *Maud Muller:* "For of all sad words of tongue or pen, the saddest are these: IT MIGHT HAVE BEEN!"

## REFERENCES

1. Allen, James E. "We Can End Juvenile Illiteracy," *Reader's Digest* (April 1970), 157-162.
2. Almy, Millie, Edward Chittender, and Paula Miller. *Young Children's Thinking.* New York: Teachers College Press, 1966.
3. Beery, Althea. "And Gladly Read," in Jane H. Catterson (Ed.), *Children and Literature.* Newark, Delaware: International Reading Association, 1970, 2.
4. Cremin, Lawrence A. "Focus on Education," *World Book Year Book,* 1970, 41-45.
5. Dechant, Emerald. "Why an Eclectic Approach in Reading Instruction?" in J. Allen Figurel (Ed.), *Vistas in Reading.* 1966 Proceedings, Volume 11, Part 1. Newark, Delaware: International Reading Association, 1967, 28-35.
6. Edinger, Lois V., and Ole Sand. "Schools for the Seventies and Beyond," *Today's Education* (September 1969), 74-75.

7. Gans, Roma. "The Effect of Current Emphases on Beginning Reading Materials and Methods on the Recognition of Individual Differences," in Mildred A. Dawson (Ed.), *Combining Research Results and Good Practices,* 1966 Proceedings, Volume 11, Part 2. Newark, Delaware: International Reading Association, 1967, 15-18.

8. Gates, Arthur I. "Teaching Reading Tomorrow," *Reading Teacher,* 23 (December 1969), 231-238.

9. Harris, Albert J. "Influences of Individual Differences on the Reading Program," in H. Alan Robinson (Ed.), *Meeting Individual Differences in Reading.* Chicago: University of Chicago Press, 1964, 17-24.

10. Kelly, Earl C. "What May We Now Believe?" *Prevention of Failure.* Washington, D.C.: Department of Elementary-Kindergarten-Nursery Education, 7-15.

11. Lee, Dorris M. *Diagnostic Teaching.* Washington, D.C.: American Association of Elementary-Kindergarten-Nursery Education, 1970.

12. MacGinitie, Walter H. "Evaluating Readiness for Learning to Read: A Critical Review and Evaluation of Research," *Reading Research Quarterly,* 4 (Spring 1969), 396-410.

# Some Personality Factors Relating to Reading

GARY D. SPENCER
Jersey City State College

HOW DOES PERSONALITY DEVELOP? For many years psychologists have felt that basic elements of personality were primarily inherited; however, Freud's statements that personality was mostly learned and almost completely formed by the age of five or six years stimulated much investigation in which many researchers (1, 4, 6, 11) verified that personality did form early, was learned, and was mostly influenced in the home (3, 5, 7, 8, 10). Symonds (10) also reviewed researches done by many and concluded that activity levels, social responsiveness, self-concept, and ego strength were the learned behaviors in personality development (9). This paper will focus on some common personality patterns and how they might influence reading.

Opposite types of personality patterns can develop and usually do exist in the classroom. The strategy in teaching these personality types is a major focus. The opposing types might best be illustrated in the form of a large semicircle representing a continuum from the extremely "compulsive" side to the opposite end representing what can be labeled the extreme "hysterical" type personality. The midpoint of this continuum would represent a neutral position or one of equal portions of both personality types and should be considered rather normal. For purposes of illustration, however, personalities more toward each end of the continuum should also be included.

## Compulsive Personality Types

The compulsive personality type person could be characterized as "cellular" or "organized" or the typical "perfectionist." Every aspect of this person's life is routinely planned and scheduled. One

**15**

can almost tell the time of day by this person's activities. His meals, his activities, his job, all are usually well organized and well planned. This personality type tends to be rather conservative in dress, authoritarian with children, and rigid about rules for himself as well as others. This person must have a planned time slot for all the activities in which he is involved or anxiety will form; and if this stress continues, more permanent tension develops and tends to negate many kinds of learning (2). This personality type can be seen in teachers who tend to follow these teaching practices: They usually hold very close to a lesson plan. They do not deviate much from it and find it frustrating to improvise when the occasion demands. The more toward the extreme end they go, the more rigidity is expressed. They like to lecture better than to discuss, and they prefer desks in a row, floors clean, and little talking. This personality type tends to gravitate toward the more specific areas of curriculum, such as the sciences, mathematics, and the social sciences.

### The Hysterical Personality Types

On the opposite end of the continuum we find a personality type called the "hysterical." One word could describe the life of this person: *chaotic.* He has all the best intentions but usually something seems to change the priorities for the day's activities. This personality type may plan to teach with a well-planned lesson; but when a pupil asks a question, the "hysterical" may leave the intended lesson and improvise a new one, keyed to the student's question. This type person tends to avoid schedules (to avoid anxiety) as much as possible and in many cases tries to destroy or nullify the scheduling activities with which he comes in contact.

### Personality Types and Child Rearing

The foregoing commonly observed adult personality patterns also tend to be applied to the children in immediate families. A compulsive parent who wants a well-organized household tends to organize the behavioral patterns of the children as well. There are usually well-enforced rules and regulations which have been imposed on the child since early childhood. The eating, work, rest, and recreation patterns are usually well organized, routine, or nonexistent. The child from a very early age is plugged into the family activities and needs not or even dares not question these rules or behavior patterns. From this type family two readily observable personality variations can be seen. They both are still compulsive types but differ greatly from each other. One is called the *independent compulsive* and the other the *dependent compulsive*. The independent compulsive is almost the image of the compulsive parent. He tends to be somewhat brighter and more verbal (especially with adults) and seeks to do his own organizing and planning for his interests. This type child often becomes the rebel at adolescence since his structure and the parents' structure often conflict.

The dependent-compulsive type child tends to be more withdrawn, passive, and less verbal than the independent-compulsive but responds to well-organized, routine, and specific goal-directed learning. He has usually been dominated, subjugated, or manipulated by the family which tends to be more authoritarian than the family which produced the independent compulsive.

Two types of "hysterical" personalities can develop. Again they conform to the general hysterical patterns but also are of *independent* and *dependent* types. The *independent-hysterical* tends to be brighter and more verbal than the *dependent-hysterical*. He has usually had substantial contact with different familial life styles and has been able to adapt himself to the chaotic nature of his surroundings. He tends to be a highly sensitive and moralistic type. This personality type has its foundations in the chaotic nonconsistent type of early childhood which resulted in a child who wants to know the answers to the riddle of life. This questioning and sensitiveness to everyone and everything will usually stay with the *independent-hysterical* throughout his life.

The *dependent-hysterical* also has his roots in the chaos of the nonstructural family; however, he has not been able to see any patterns to life, and thus he becomes quite fearful of it. As a result, he begins to shrink from the reality of life and withdraws from it into his own dream world. A large percentage of psychotic children could come from this personality type.

## Personality Types and Teachers

All of the personality types discussed are easily seen in the classroom if one observes them closely; however, the personality type of the teacher is not easily observed. More important is how it influences the type of instruction given and the responses expected from children. The majority of classroom teachers by the very process of having to pursue the many years of school and college to become teachers usually have to fall somewhat past the center of the continuum toward the "compulsive" side. This teacher quite often perpetuates this cycle by giving instruction in such a way that the compulsive child is more easily rewarded and thus becomes the successful student on his way to higher education.

The individual differences in personality of children are just as important as the differences of intelligence, language, or experience.

## Personality and Reading Instruction

Since personality permeates every action and every aspect of our lives, it is only natural that it should affect learning and the way youngsters learn to read.

For the *independent-compulsive,* the child is the organizer (and the manipulator) of his school environment. When a teacher is not specific or directive enough, this child will tend to organize the situation through questions or subtle statements. He generally is quite verbal, and with a compulsive teacher the child is considered a good student. The deficiencies, however, are ones of lack of decision making abilities, lack of creative initiative, and some loss of aesthetic appreciation (such as literature or poetry appreciation) in the language arts. If this child is placed in a nondirected or qualitative situation, anxiety can produce a lack of learning or even an inability to use previous learning. More explicitly, the gap between what he prefers (well-organized routines) and what he needs (more flexibility and adaptability) can be filled with activities such as language experience activity, literature appreciation, creative writing activities, and contextual vocabulary. The foregoing should produce good tolerance of less rigid aspects of this world.

For the *dependent-compulsive* child, however, things are quite different. This personality has been controlled and manipulated during his early life to the extent that he wants to be told how, when, or what to do. Again this knowledge gives us the strategy for instruction. This child should be given as much structure as is necessary to allow him to succeed but always moving past the threshold toward more decision making, more responsibilities, more initiative, and especially toward more self-directed activities.

Specific activities might include concrete comprehension skill activities that become more abstract, art work as a comprehension technique, specific vocabulary meanings moving toward multiple meanings which he must create, deciding how long a research report should be, and making outlines and summaries of books he has liked.

The *independent-hysterical* child has developed a personality that helps him to cope with very chaotic situations, to improvise, and to desire learning about everything. He quite often is deficient in the organizational patterns of learning and in the endurance or diligence necessary to stay with a dull or routine (to him) but necessary activity.

Quite often this personality type gets overinvolved in too many activities to do justice to any of them. This information should lead the teacher to strategies that permit creativeness and initiative but that also require some acceptance of highly structured, less interesting, drill-type, or time consuming long term projects that cannot be completed at one sitting. These can be accomplished by the involvement of the child in creative writing or research projects that have subparts and demand revision or rewriting. Art projects, phonics skills, vocabulary building, and spelling exercises provide the routine and structured activities that will build more tolerance of the needed structure.

The remaining personality type, the *dependent-hysterical,* is perhaps the most difficult to work with because of the basic shyness and withdrawn character. This child will not pursue learning but will daydream or attempt to escape the learning situation by crying, avoiding, or just plain sitting and waiting for teacher. He usually likes to draw, tell tall tales, sing or play music; and these activities can usually be used as motivators for learning other things. It is very important for this child to have personal instruction as he feels more confident with it and responds well to this type of approach. This fact may explain some of the dramatic increases that result when youngsters are placed in remedial reading (one-to-one or small groups). A balance is necessary between skill building that is routine and, therefore, less frightening and involvement in more game-type and motivating-type activities to reach the less concrete or apparent reading skills.

This paper has tried to show how personalities of both teacher and pupil are related to reading and learning. The writer would be the first to say that the model presents a neat, concise description of some obvious types of personality differences which, in actuality, are never pure. Also the multiplicity of variables that affect personality development—such as the first-born child vs. the youngest in the family; two radically different personality types in the home; traumatic shocks in early life such as divorce, deaths, severe physical illness, and mental illness—can never be static. Mischel (5) states it well when he says, "We do need to recognize that discontinuities . . . are part of the genuine phenomena of personality."

REFERENCES

1. Cronbach, Lee J. "The Two Disciplines of Scientific Psychology," *American Psychologist,* 55 (December 1957), 671-684.
2. Fleishman, E. A., and G. D. Ellison. "Prediction of Transfer and Other Learning from Ability and Personality Measures," *Journal of Educational Psychology,* 60 (August 1969), 300-313.
3. Jones, Earnst. "Freud Psychology," *Psychological Bulletin,* 7 (February 1911), 109-128.
4. Melton, A. W. "Individual Differences and Theoretical Process Variables," in R. M. Gagne (Ed.), *Learning and Individual Differences.* Columbus, Ohio: Merrill, 1967.

5. Mischel, Walter. "Continuity and Change in Personality," *American Psychologist,* 24 (November 1969), 1012-1018.

6. Owens, W. A. "Toward One Discipline of Scientific Psychology," *American Psychologist,* 23 (1968), 782-785.

7. Ribble, Margaret. *The Rights of Infants.* New York: Columbia Press, 1943.

8. Sears, Roy, E. E. Macroby, and Harry Levin. *Patterns of Child Rearing.* New York: Row, Peterson, 1957.

9. Symonds, Percival M. *What Education Has to Learn from Psychology.* New York: Columbia University Press, 1960.

10. Symonds, Percival M. *The Psychology of Parent-Child Relationships.* New York: Appleton-Century, 1939.

11. Vale, James R., and Carole Vale. "Individual Differences and General Laws in Psychology: a Reconciliation," *American Psychologist,* 24 (December 1969), 1093-1108.

# Classroom Organization in Meeting Individual Needs

JERRY CONVERSE
Delaware Department of Public Instruction

THE PURPOSE of this paper is to explain how teachers might organize the classroom to meet the language development needs of students by the establishment of multigroup or individualized instruction through a number of learning centers.

One of the most difficult aspects of organizing centers is helping the teacher plan in terms of varying responsibilities for directing classroom activities. Teacher-directed activities must be kept at a minimum so that the teacher will have enough time to supervise the overall operations in the room. Semidirected activities allow the teacher to conduct a portion of the lesson (the readiness or follow up to a story) but place most of the responsibility for the lesson on the learner. Student-directed activities, such as one-to-one reading, library research, and a buddy-buddy spelling program, put limited restrictions on the teacher's time. Self-directed activities also permit the teacher the greatest freedom.

## Listening Center

With little effort and minimal preparation the teacher can involve a group of students in the listening center while she is free for other instructional activities. Much of the equipment that a teacher needs for a listening center in her room is readily available. The record player, tape recorder, and filmstrip projector are generally standard equipment in schools. If instructional television (ITV) is available, it, too, can become a part of the listening center.

The teacher can close off a section of the room for her listening center by shifting classroom furniture. She might use the table which holds the tape recorder, record player, and listening post as part of the inside "wall" of the listening center. By putting the front of the TV set to the inside of the listening center, the teacher can use the back of the set and its stand as another part of the "wall." Teachers have used portable chalkboards, movable bulletin boards, or room dividers for the same purpose.

The teacher can choose from a variety of motivational and instructional programs. For reading motivation she might select from programs (20, 11, 15, 16, 22) which use combinations of records, tapes, books, and filmstrips to interest children in reading. For developing phonic skills the teacher might choose from record, standard tape, or cassette programs like those developed by Brake (3), Packer and Boag (13), and others. For developing listening skills, the teacher might choose the Bracken (2) listening-skills-builder program. Or, she might prefer to tape the listening exercises from the Parker materials (14) to teach TQLR skills in her listening center.

If a teacher uses ITV as a part of her listening center program, it can become the stimulus for many learning activities. Programs which are directly related to reading include Listen and Say (12), Quest for the Best (10), Wordsmith (18), and Biography (9). Content programs like Places in the News or The Adventures of Science (4), can be used for developing the language skills of oral or written reports, sharing ideas in discussion, and stimulating library research.

## The Self-Selection Center

As she does in the listening center, the teacher can develop the self-selection reading center with little effort and minimal planning. She needs a place to display materials for the children to read. Then, once she teaches the students when and how to use the center, it becomes primarily self-directed.

The materials for this center might include trade books, unused basal readers, magazines, and newspapers. Since Barbe (1), Veatch (21), and others have written extensively on establishing the classroom library for an individualized reading program, it is not necessary to do so here.

When the pupil has chosen a book to read from the self-selection area, the library, or from his own personal collection, he should apply the reading skills he has learned elsewhere. The teacher, in checking to see that he is doing so, might test the following: 1) Has the child set purposes for his reading? 2) Has he surveyed the material in preparation for reading it? 3) Does he readjust his predictions as he reads? 4) Does he use his word attack skills, context clues, or other word-gathering devices? and 5) Is he developing a vocabulary from the new words encountered in his reading material?

## Skills Center

If materials are available in the classroom for skills development, teachers can easily establish a skills center, which is simply an area for storing such matter. The skills center should include materials which offer the student an opportunity for additional practice in reading skills, such as the workbooks which accompany the basal reader, phonic workbooks and games, skill building kits, "The Spectrum of Skills" (8), *Reading Pacemaker Kits* (6), the *Reading for Meaning Series* (7), the *Be a Better Reader Series* (17), and many more.

Teachers will determine which skill exercises might help the student, and they will observe him during the directed reading-thinking lessons or self-selection checks. If he displays a reading weakness which can be self-corrected in the skills program, the teacher will assign the appropriate lessons. If it is a skill that must be taught, she will do so and provide extra practice to reinforce the skill. In either case the teacher performs minimal supervision while the student learns in the skills center.

With the classroom organization that develops from a learning-centers program, the teacher can also introduce a differentiated-level spelling approach. The individualized spelling approach is most effective when the pupils use a buddy-buddy system.

One teacher in Delaware has her spelling program organized in the following manner. Each day when it is time for spelling, half of the class (one member of each partnership) goes to the skills area in the room to get the spelling lists. After these pupils have returned to their seats, the other half choose spelling lists for their member in the partnership. For the next five minutes the students dictate the words to their partners. Each student then takes his own spelling list and checks his work for errors. In a systematic manner the pupil marks off the words he has just been tested on, makes a record of his errors, practices the words he missed, and takes a retest of the words he missed in that lesson. In this particular system the missed words are reviewed after 24 hours, after one week, and at the end of the month.

Students who develop their word attack, comprehension, and spelling skills in the manner described, develop a feeling of independence and self-reliance. They become adept at identifying skill deficiencies, at locating the material which will help them overcome these deficiencies, and in working with the materials. If the pupils want to learn, they no longer need to wait until the teacher is ready to teach them.

## Writing Center

Unlike the other centers in the room, the writing center is more a method of teaching writing skills than a location in the room. The teacher might use composition skillbooks or books from the self-selection center to teach writing skills.

According to Burrows (5) and others, the best written language follows from an experience and oral discussion. In the writing-center lesson the teacher might direct an experience with the children on one day. The group would then discuss the experience, at which time oral language development, concept development, and vocabulary development would be emphasized. Following the extensive discussion, the pupils would write about their experience.

Later the teacher may select a few compositions and make a transparency of each. Using the transparencies to discuss the strength of each composition, the teacher emphasizes the pieces of good writing, rather than having each child focus on red-penciled errors.

Each member of the group edits his own composition in relation to those which were projected. The teacher tells the student to prepare the assignment again and imitate the positive features of the composition discussed. She reads the composition and comments on it only after each child has edited and rewritten his work.

## Directed Reading Center

Stauffer (19) writes about the principles and boundaries of the group-directed reading-thinking activities. Essentially, he says that the group offers each of its members a chance to share common materials for the purpose of developing reading-thinking skills by having the students share in setting purposes, weighing evidence, seeking answers to their own questions, adjusting purposes, and proving points. In the joint effort the students learn from one another; the teacher plays a secondary role of "intellectual agitator."

During the directed reading-thinking lesson the teacher observes how each student uses reading-thinking skills. Can he set an appropriate purpose? Does he get his answer? Can he prove it? Does he use the table of contents, glossary, and index when he should? Does he use appropriate word attack skills? Has he learned the "new" words of the story? Can he interpret figurative language? Can he differentiate between fact and opinion? Can he recall the events of the story sequentially? The teacher then uses her observations to plan how to help students overcome their reading-thinking deficiencies.

The teacher has several options for correcting a skill deficiency. When it is a minor one, she may assign appropriate self-corrective exercises in the skills center. If the deficiency is more serious, however, she may carefully guide the student(s) through the exercises in the skills center; or she might use a group-directed reading lesson to teach the skill, before letting the students use the skills center for additional practice.

This unusual way to use the directed reading center in a classroom calls for a rather sophisticated teacher. To be successful in this type of program the teacher must know a sequence of reading skills, assess skill deficiencies accurately, and teach the skills that the student needs to read for information and for pleasure.

## Other Centers

Depending on the age of her pupils, the teacher might select other centers for the classroom. She could use an oral-language-development center to house puppets, framing devices (such as a stage or TV set), flannelboards, pictures to stimulate oral language, stories and plays to be acted out, and poems for choral reading. The teacher might also set up a games center for phonic games, checkers, jigsaw puzzles, spill and spell, password, and concentration. Possibilities for other centers in the room are limited only by the teacher's imagination for establishing a purpose and by the space and materials available.

## Conclusion

The teacher has an unusual role in the classroom described here. Her primary duty is not to perform from the center of the stage for a captive audience nor to impart information. After creating a stimulating environment for her pupils, the teacher's concern is to guide them carefully through the experiences and exercises which will not only develop reading skills but will also encourage the pupils to seek information and pleasure through reading.

REFERENCES

1. Barbe, Walter B. *Educator's Guide to Personalized Reading Instruction.* Englewood Cliffs, New Jersey: Prentice Hall, 1961.
2. Bracken, Dorothy K. *Listening Skills Program.* Chicago: Science Research Associates, 1969.
3. Brake, Rachel G. *Phonics Skilltapes Series.* Columbus, Ohio: Charles E. Merrill, 1968.
4. Burns, John W. *The Adventures of Science* (Teacher's Guide). Lafayette, Indiana: Midwest Program on Airborne Television Instruction, 1962.
5. Burrows, Alvina T., et al. *They All Want to Write.* Englewood Cliffs, New Jersey: Prentice Hall, 1952.
6. Cohen, S. Alan. *Reading Pacemaker Kits.* New York: Random House, 1968.
7. Coleman, John, and Ann Jungeblut. *Reading for Meaning Series.* New York: Lippincott, 1965.

8. Deighton, L., et al. *The Macmillan Reading Spectrum*. New York: Macmillan, 1963.
9. Delaware Educational Television Network. *Biography* (Teacher's Guide). Dover, Delaware: Delaware Educational Television Network, 1970.
10. Denver Public Schools. *Quest for the Best Children's Literature Series*. Denver: Denver Public Schools, 1964.
11. Kidder, Robert. *Sights and Sounds Learning Units*. New York: Random House, 1969.
12. Miner, Adah. *Listen and Say* (Teacher's Guide). Lafayette, Indiana: Midwest Program on Airborne Television, 1964.
13. Packer, Athol, and Audrey K. Boag (Advisors). *Imperial Primary Reading Program*. Kankakee, Illinois: Imperial International Learning, 1968.
14. Parker, Donald. *SRA Reading Lab IIIA*. Chicago: Science Research Associates, 1967.
15. Pines, Mark. *Honey Power*. Altadena, California: Lyceum Productions, 1969.
16. Rydell, Wendy. *Image Makers*. New York: Eye Gate House, 1969.
17. Smith, Nila Banton. *Be a Better Reader Series*. Englewood Cliffs, New Jersey: Prentice Hall, 1969.
18. Smith, Robert W. L. *The Wordsmith* (Teacher's Guide). Bloomington, Indiana: National Center for School and College Television.
19. Stauffer, Russell G. *Directing Reading Maturity as a Cognitive Process*. New York: Harper and Row, 1969.
20. Storm, Doris. *Footprints on the Moon*. Pleasantville, New Jersey: Guidance Assoc./Harcourt Brace, 1969.
21. Veatch, Jeannette. *Individualizing Your Reading Program*. New York: Putnam, 1959.
22. Young, Wm. E., B. Leary, and E. A. Myers. *Reading Skilltapes Series*. Columbus, Ohio: Charles E. Merrill.

# Reading in a Family-Grouped Primary School

ELISABETH WATTERS
Windermere School, Beaconsfield, Quebec

BEFORE DESCRIBING family grouping, a brief account of the community background for our experiment seems to be indicated. Windermere School was scheduled to be built in a new section of Beaconsfield, an area near Montreal, which has grown quite phenomenally in the past 25 years. The plans for the new school were the most modern possible, and the intention was to incorporate an open-area building with team teaching and a nongraded school. The staff was recruited on the basis of their interest in teaching along the foregoing lines and was divided into primary, intermediate, and senior teams. This paper is concerned with the activities of the primary team in which six teachers were responsible for 180 children of five, six, and seven years of age. Since we were to begin in a new school with exceptional facilities with no need to restructure old patterns, we were eager to select an approach that did not box the children into a graded system, even though some of the older ones had already experienced it.

To explore some of these approaches first hand, I went to England in the spring preceding our opening, where I was able, through the interest and cooperation of the Director of the Institute of Education at Reading, to visit thirteen infant schools and three training colleges. What I saw, backed up by specific reading, influenced me in favor of family grouping. I found desirable qualities in the children: They were friendly, communicative, and eager to show me what they were doing and appeared very mature in their independence, resourcefulness, and mutual understanding. They were engaged in a variety of interesting projects which they were able to organize and to write about at a high level of achievement. I was surprised when the age range was pointed out to me as it was not immediately apparent in the way the children worked and played together.

29

The age range is the basic feature of family grouping, also called vertical age grouping. A child remains in one class during the period of his primary school life; his progress occurs within the framework of that class; all classes are organized in the same way and have equal status. By avoiding the annual transfer of children, the possibilities of giving far better individual care and instruction seem much greater. If the ages five, six, and seven are included in the parallel classes, each teacher loses one-third of a class each year and takes in one-third of a class of new and unknown children. It is our belief that the return to school in the fall should be a much easier and more relaxed experience for those children who do not have to move to a new class with a new teacher.

We had the opportunity to watch the effects of the mutual aid which the children give to each other, such as the six-year-old, just past the stage of beginning reading, who appeared with two five-year-olds and announced "You know what? Rob and Stevie can read—I just taught them." This is not to say that they really could read, but it is evidence of a positive attitude toward reading that is common in our classes. Another five-year-old liked to solve the problems in math stories when they were read to him by an older child who had considerable difficulty in seeing through them himself, even though he could read the words. One highly intelligent six-year-old rejected all sorts of approaches to beginning reading. On the Stanford Primary 1 he scored only 1.6 on word reading and 1.3 on paragraph reading, though on the vocabulary section he scored among the highest in the school. Just recently a solution was found: he takes a library book into the hallway, arranges the very youngest five-year-olds sitting along the wall, places himself firmly in a chair before them, and reads to them with all the dramatic expression of a Shakespearian actor—and they listen to him!

In addition to the mutual aid which seems to come about as the result of the mixed ages in the family-grouped classes, we feel that the stable relationship with the teacher, built up over a longer period than one school year, will prove to be valuable to young children.

Our decision to adopt family grouping developed from a series of summer meetings when it became clear that we felt one of our prime educational aims was to help children become independent and self-directing. This goal would lead to their being better equipped to use their later education than children who were the products of a traditional approach with its emphasis on content and the memorization of facts, rules, and processes. Because we wanted to provide an environment which included opportunities for emotional, social, and intellectual growth, we reasoned that in a family-grouped class the children who developed unevenly would always be able to find the level which was most appropriate to them. We felt that family grouping was better for a slow child if the difference between his achievement and that of others in the class could be minimized; family grouping offered an easier way to accomplish the foregoing.

Obviously one of our more specific aims is that children should read well. Since the skills of language as forms of communication are inseparable, conversation is largely continuous. Writing, in the form of book-making, has been encouraged from the beginning, in class books and individual books, as well as in scrapbooks arranged and pasted by younger children and captioned by older ones. We feel that the children's attitude toward reading is important and that it is valuable for beginners to see learning going on all around them. "I can't read that very well yet but I will soon" is a common reaction to the appearance of a new book in the reading corner, rather than "I can't read that. I haven't learned the words." Ideally, we would combine reading with language and interest work, though we freely admit that we are unable to do this all the time. We have taken comfort from the statement of a principal who said "All teachers, however long they have taught, appear inexperienced when they first start family grouping. The ability to cope successfully with it appears to lie in the attitude towards it more than actual teaching experience."

We agreed that we wanted to emphasize learning to read rather than the teaching of reading and to resist the pressures of the past which caused many children to be pushed through the books of a graded basal series. We decided that we would use a wide variety of materials. We did not feel that we had to commit ourselves to either individualized reading or ability grouping but rather that our program should provide opportunities for both.

We have tried to accept the fact that we are wrong when we think children are learning only when we are actively engaged in teaching them. We do not interpret this statement to mean that there should be little or no systematic teaching of reading but rather the teaching should not precede the reading as it so often does. We prefer the idea that active teaching is best given when children are reading from a book, rather than in isolated lessons, or in preparing for a story by solving all possible difficulties before they have been encountered by the children. We have also entertained the notion that perhaps the teaching of reading is not such a difficult and complicated matter as we have been led to believe, and as we have, in turn, led children to feel that it is. Problems we encountered in the past may often have been of our own making.

Because reading for meaning should become a habit rather than a skill to be taught, from the beginning we have emphasized that the children should expect all reading to make sense. We also do not feel that it is necessary to keep a child reading one book until he knows every word in it. Some of the seven-year-olds have chosen to read a rather difficult third grade book and have made quite mature observations on the need for going slowly in order to understand. Because one scientific extract defeated them, it was read aloud to them. When they still could not grasp it, we simply dropped it. The important thing was that they themselves recognized that they were not getting the meaning.

Some description of the materials, other than basal readers, is essential to an understanding of our approach. We ordered a large number of "little" books, for which the children have shown much enthusiasm. Even the five-year-olds experienced a sense of achievement from reading the many caption books, though they were not reading in the fullest sense.

We color-coded these books with strips of tape and had a variety of reading material that presented very little difficulty at every stage. When beginning readers could not unlock words they had not seen before, they asked someone. The teacher observed that when the children next met the word, they read it at sight. Because many of the words were peculiar to Britain, some interesting phonics discussions took place, such as, "It's a picture of a truck, but it doesn't say truck; the sounds are wrong." The printed word, of course, was *lorry*. The caption books had a hidden value when the older children discovered that they could serve as picture dictionaries.

We used a programed approach to teach letter sounds and blending. Simple games, designed to teach initial consonants, were popular with five-year-olds, who learned to associate pictures of objects with letter forms through playing with the cards in their own way. Only a small gap was left to be bridged when they later played according to the rules of identifying an object by the sound of its initial consonant. Older children directed the more complicated games and received practice that they particularly needed.

Our daily program is generally unstructured. With no set approach to the teaching of reading, we have found it unnecessary to schedule time for the usual group sessions. The reading achievement of older children was assessed at the beginning of the year on the basis of past records and present performance. Though the children were at first fascinated by the little books, they soon ran through these and chose both basal readers and workbooks for regular work, indicating quite plainly that they wanted the security of this type of book. Guidelines were planned so that the children understood they were expected to read regularly and record what they had read. On the basis of these records small groups were, and continue to be, drawn out for specific instruction. Sometimes this instruction is concerned with reading skills, and sometimes a story is chosen for a directed reading lesson with particular emphasis on thinking ahead and more sophisticated interpretation. Children regularly read orally to the teacher and frequently to each other and to small groups of younger children from books of their choice. Evaluation is achieved by means of anecdotal records and informal inventories, rather than tests. While this plan may appear to be somewhat less than an accurate measurement of reading achievement, we are finding that we have developed an understanding of each child's "reading personality." In many cases we have helped the child to a better understanding of himself.

Those who began the year as nonreaders were encouraged to regard reading as a natural thing which they would soon be able to do. As well as using the little books, they saw their own words written by the teacher and were encouraged to write "stories" of their own. For example, the book *What I Like* led to many pictures captioned "I like _____," the missing word often being supplied by an older child. When they wanted basal readers for themselves, these were supplied; several children read straight through the first preprimers with very little help. Others have started very slowly and a few have not started at all. Some five-year-olds have joined the readers on their own volition, and some have not shown the slightest interest. At the present time all who can read are using basal readers, library books, activity books, reference books, teacher-made assignment cards, and reading games. We feel that we have succeeded in avoiding the stigma of the bottom group and have, to a considerable degree, weaned both ourselves and the children away from the artificial standards of the conventional grades.

The teachers participating in the experiment thought that some attempt should be made to assess progress in terms of a standardized test; therefore, the Primary 1 and 2 batteries of the Stanford Achievement Test were used. No attempt at statistical analysis is offered, but the results were generally satisfactory and appeared to indicate that the reading had not suffered from the overall approach of vertical age grouping.

We feel that the advantages or disadvantages of family grouping, with specific reference to reading, cannot become fully apparent in one year. Working with the very young five-year-olds has proved difficult; as our system allows for only half days for kindergarten, we are considering removing them from the group next year. Some whole group activities may have suffered, but we hope through better planning and better use of the special talents of various staff members to improve these in the future. All of us agree that this type of class has given us unusual opportunities to observe the growth and development of children and to recognize a wider range of individual differences. Many opinions, which have been voiced by other teachers who have worked with family grouping for a number of years, indicate that its long range values are worthwhile. The comments with which we felt we were most qualified to agree after one year were the following: "Children are more involved with their own progress." "No sense of one class being inferior or superior to another." "Working with children of all ages is more intellectually satisfying for the teacher." We have not tried to change just because change is the fashion but rather because we were dissatisfied with some of the things we saw happening to children in existing situations. We are far from satisfied with what we have accomplished to date, but we did not expect to be fully satisfied. The proof of the pudding is in the eating, and we have only begun to nibble.

# Personalized Reading Progress— Multi-Aged Nongrading

ANN POLLARD WILLIAMSON
Corsicana, Texas, Schools

EDUCATORS, more especially teachers of reading, have been committed to the idea of personalizing instruction for over half a century. Innovative attempts in the past have included interest and ability grouping, tutoring, unit teaching, team teaching, and flexible scheduling. Some of the more recent attempts have included programed instruction, computer-based instruction (9), individual contracts (7), and individually prescribed instruction (2). Educators and researchers continue the odyssey to find a satisfying solution to the age-old problem—making reading instruction relevant to the needs of each child.

Personalized reading progress—or its variations of individualized reading, self-selection in reading, and individually prescribed instruction—has as its basis the attempt to tailor the reading program to the achievement and rate of development of the individual learner. It carries with it the idea of student participation in decision making about his reading materials to assure relevance. Students are given more freedom and more responsibility for the learning process than they might be given in other programs.

The idea of individualizing instruction is universally appealing, but the attempts of actual implementation have been meager. Recently, however, educators have begun to feel a new urgency about the problem. We may actually be entering a new era of research and technology which will afford at least partial solutions to diagnosing and prescribing individual programs geared to the interests, needs, and abilities of each child.

Proponents of nongradedness state that grouping by chronological age for instruction is no more feasible than grouping by shoe size. Remember Procrustes? He was the mythological Greek robber who placed all his victims on a standard sized bed. If they were too long for it, he simply chopped them down to size. For those too short, he stretched them until they fit. For years in the history of education we have forced our "victims" into the same mold by either stretching or chopping them to fit the curriculum.

Nongrading has attempted to take the masses out of the mold. What exactly is nongrading? "It is both an organizational structure and a philosophical, educational position. Organizationally, grade lines and grade designations have been removed, and there are many organizational patterns or nongradedness. Philosophically, nongradedness is an approach in working with students so that each child may grow and develop at his own pace and on his own level" (5).

Without grade level designations in reading, the teacher must be especially flexible and adaptable in locating material and developing methods with which to work with students. "The idea is to schedule learning at the student's past accomplishment level and to feed ideas and learning at the individual student's level of understanding" (4). For example, in a typical third grade class, there are probably the extremes of a few nonreaders to those students reading on the sixth or seventh grade level. If the teacher places all children in third grade readers, the bright ones coast along, probably never being challenged, while the nonreaders become more frustrated each day with continual failure and lowering of self-esteem.

In a nongraded reading situation, the bright child will be challenged to his potential while the slower reader will be placed where he can perform successfully. When he is able to succeed, he develops reading skills sequentially. Although nongrading has received much attention in the past decade, it is actually not a new concept for reading teachers, for good teachers of reading have always attempted to provide reading experiences which will result in a feeling of satisfaction and success for each student. In order to achieve this attitude, the individual student is accepted at his reading level and motivated and accelerated to a rate of progress compatible with his potential.

**Where Do We Begin?**

In the fall of 1970, Corsicana Comprehensive High School in Corsicana, Texas, opened a new building, original in design and function and operating entirely on a nongraded basis. Corsicana educators, realizing that the teaching of reading skills cannot terminate with elementary school nor even the middle school, for the first time established a reading department at the secondary level. Reading personnel were challenged with the task of setting up a secondary reading program using the nongraded approach. They were told that the reading classes would be composed of multi-aged, multilevel pupils with a reading achievement span of perhaps ten years within a given class.

The logical place to begin was the development of a curriculum guide in which objectives were stated in a pattern of skill development. The following skills pyramid was established:

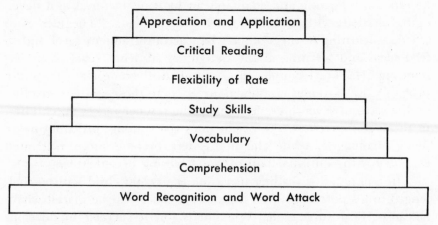

Appreciation and Application

Critical Reading

Flexibility of Rate

Study Skills

Vocabulary

Comprehension

Word Recognition and Word Attack

Each of the skills on the pyramid was further broken down into subskills. It should be stated here that although the skills are listed in a somewhat sequential pattern, they are not necessarily hierarchical in nature. The word recognition and word attack skill level has been put at the base of the pyramid because it is fundamental to all the others. Personalized reading progress demands that the student be "plugged in" at any level of the skill development pyramid in which he shows a deficiency.

## Selection of Materials

The second step in the establishment of a secondary nongraded, multi-aged reading program is the selection of necessary materials for personalizing instruction. Because of the diversity of abilities, interests, and needs in a given class, materials of a broad range of interest and difficulty must be provided. The concept of a single text-book has long ago yielded to the multilevel, multisensory types of materials. The adjustment of materials and methods to meet individual differences in reading abilities is one of the most difficult problems the teacher faces. With a great variety of materials from which to select, the teacher is better able to meet this task.

Multilevel materials for both elementary and secondary schools are available in such great abundance that the problem is not in locating them as in former times but in evaluating and selecting those which best fit the needs of the local program.

## Diagnosis

In order to know at what level to place the individual student, a procedure for diagnosis of student achievement in terms of the objectives of the curriculum must be implemented. Included in diagnosis in the Corsicana program will be the informal inventories, survey tests, diagnostic reading tests, and interest inventories. Information in the cumulative folder including estimated capacity, vision and hearing, and past performance will be noted. Interviews with the teachers, parents, and peers may reveal helpful information.

Diagnosis is basic in developing a personalized approach to reading. This initial period of diagnosis will be followed by continuously diagnosing individual achievement throughout the year.

## Individual Prescription

With the realization that each pupil is unique in ability, interests, and needs and that there are methods and materials available for all levels of these abilities, interests, and needs, the problem then becomes one of individually prescribing a program of instruction for each pupil. This is perhaps the most difficult of all the steps in setting up the personalized approach.

After listing the individual's strengths and weaknesses according to diagnosis, taking into account interests and background, a personalized program of instruction is written allowing options for individual choice by the pupil. In a conference between the teacher and pupil, the teacher discusses frankly and openly the latter's need for intensive instruction in certain areas. The pupil is offered choices in the materials he feels will be most relevant for him. Thus, by employing him in the decision making process of his personalized program, he is given some of the responsibility for his own learning.

This type of individual prescription may, on the surface, seem time consuming and impractical for a teacher who is assigned several classes each day. With the increased use of paraprofessionals and with the promise of computer-assisted instruction, such individualization can become a reality.

## Total School Environment

In the Corsicana program, plans are being made for the pupil to utilize his newly acquired reading skills in other subject areas. Close cooperation will exist between departments as the reading teachers report an individual's progress in reading to his English, history, math, and science teachers. Suggestions will be made to these content area teachers concerning materials which might enhance the student's understanding of the subject content.

## Continuous Evaluation

In order to assure personalized reading progress in this multi-aged, nongraded program, there must be constant evaluation both of the total reading program and of each individual's progress. It is imperative that accurate records of diagnosis, prescription, and evaluation be kept. In the Corsicana program, plans are being implemented for statistical analyses of both individual progress and total program development. Variables such as diagnostic instruments, pupil interest and progress, effectiveness of materials used, and carryover of reading skills into content areas will be evaluated.

Continuous inservice work for teachers and administrators of the program will continue to be held for exchange of ideas and information, with attention being given to the direction of research in other schools. Technological developments are reviewed, and their effects on personalized instruction are evaluated and utilized when applicable.

## Advantages of Personalized Reading Progress

The advantages of personalized reading progress for the pupil appear to be the following: It enables him to proceed at his own pace; it permits him to have a one-to-one relationship with the teacher; it gives him feelings of success and self-esteem; it allows him to take some responsibility in his own learning; and it gives him freedom in selection of materials.

For the teacher the advantages of the personalized reading progress include the following: It enables him to meet more accurately the personalized needs of each child; it furnishes him with diagnostic devices; it allows him to spend more time with students who need help the most; it enables him to bring a structured, carefully thought out program to his pupils; it brings a higher degree of job satisfaction; and it changes his role to that of a director of learning.

Personalized reading instruction offers promise of breaking through to the individual—perhaps the fulfillment of a promise long overdue in the teaching of reading.

REFERENCES AND NOTES

1. Barbe, Walter B. *Educator's Guide to Personalized Reading Instruction.* Englewood Cliffs, New Jersey: Prentice-Hall, 1961.
2. Beck, Isabel L., and John O. Bolvin. "A Model for Nongradedness: The Reading Program for Individually Prescribed Instruction," *Elementary English,* 46 (February 1969), 130-135.
3. Blake, Howard E., and Ann W. McPherson. "Individualized Instruction: Where Are We?" *Educational Technology,* 9 (December 1969), 63-65.
4. Brown, B. Frank. *The Appropriate Placement School: A Sophisticated Nongraded Curriculum.* West Nyack, New York: Parker, 1965.
5. Casavis, James N. "Nongradedness: A Formula for Change," *New York State Education,* 57 (December 1969), 22-23.

6. Della-Piana, Gabriel. *Reading Diagnosis and Prescription*. New York: Holt, Rinehart and Winston, 1968.

7. Esbensen, Thowald. "Student Learning Contracts: The Duluth Model," *Educational Screen and Audiovisual Guide,* 47 (January 1969), 16-17.

8. Frazier, Alexander. "Individualized Instruction," *Educational Leadership,* 25 (April 1968), 616-624.

9. Holden, George S. "The Effects of Computer Based Resource Units Upon Instructional Behavior," *Journal of Experimental Education,* 36 (Spring 1969), 27-30.

10. Hunt, Lyman C., Jr. (Ed.). *The Individualized Reading Program: A Guide for Classroom Teachers,* 1966 Proceedings, Volume 11, Part 3. Newark, Delaware: International Reading Association, 1967.

11. Ramsey, Wallace (Ed.). *Organizing for Individual Differences,* Perspectives in Reading No. 9. Newark, Delaware: International Reading Association, 1967.

12. Spache, George D. *Toward Better Reading*. Champaign, Illinois: Garrard, 1963, 150-166.

13. Spalding, Robert L. "Personalized Education in Southside School," *Elementary School Journal,* 70 (January 1970), 180-189.

14. Wolfson, Bernice. "Pupil and Teacher Roles in Individual Instruction," *Elementary School Journal,* 49 (April 1968), 357-366.

15. Zahorik, John A. "Individual Instruction and Group Instruction: A Case Study," *Journal of Educational Research,* 42 (July-August 1969), 453-455.

# Updating the Individual Approach to Reading:

IPI or IRP?

LYMAN C. HUNT, JR.
University of Vermont

ARE THE SIMILARITIES evoked by the *I* in both cryptic symbols of IPI and IRP more pronounced than the differences? IPI and IRP are not merely two different versions of the same basic concept. Whether reference is made to IPI or to IRP makes a difference, and the significance of the difference lies in the *P* of IPI. Is your first reaction to *P* the word *"prescribed"?* or does the *P* make you think of *"personalized"* reading instruction?

Many within the profession have not sorted out confusions which result from referring to individualized instruction, whether it be prescribed or personal, as one and the same. To use *prescribed* and *personalized* interchangeably perpetuates existing confusions. Consequently, clarification is needed.

Individually prescribed instruction (IPI) expresses the qualities and values which are usually associated with the cognitive domain. By contrast the personal part of the individual reading program (IRP) is representative of values found within affective domain. Neither one is a pure form, and the intent is not to so imply. Nor are they opposites. In actual school practice the two are usually well combined. Rather, differentiating prescribed and personalized instruction is a matter of degree. However, the differences in emphasis are very real, and it is valuable to highlight them. These contrasts can perhaps best be shown in the following form:

DISTINGUISHING CHARACTERISTICS

| *Prescribed Instruction* | *Personalized Instruction* |
|---|---|
| IPI | IRP |
| 1. Continuous Progress | 1. Discovery Learning |
| 2. Skill Mastering | 2. Learning to Learn |

3. Subject Matter Achievement
4. Programed or Compu-
terized Instruction
5. Systems Analysis
6. Behavioral Objectives

3. Personal Growth

4. Self-direction

5. Individual Productivity
6. Self-selection

## The Nature of Structure

In most IPI programs the detailed comprehensive and systematic structure is highly visible in the materials and the manuals. The same may be said of the typical basal reading series which in reality is a version of programed or prescribed instruction. The fact of structure is self-evident.

Perhaps this analogy will help. Prescribed instruction can be likened to a section of a railroad track with the initial and terminal points well marked. One can recall walking the endless series of ties, the small steps evenly spaced. One is immediately aware of any false step, catching the foot between the ties yet easily scrambling back up to take the next intervalled step. The steps are small, equally easy to take so that steady progress can be made toward the end point. One knows where he is going, and the steps needed to reach the destination are clearly marked in programed or prescribed instruction although they are individually completed.

By contrast IRP can be thought of more in the image of a cobweb: a series of concentric circles interlaced by fine lines or strands extending to outer circles. The concept is one of continuously moving outward, multidimensionally from an inner core. The idea is one of increasing increments of expansion in several directions. The implication of exploration is inherent in the concept. The straight line rule does not apply in this setting.

The contention that IRP is unstructured is not true. This structure, however, is much more in the teacher's mind than in the teacher's manual. The secret is transferring the structure from the mind of the teacher to the mind of the child. Unless the structure is clear and constant for the teacher, she will be less than successful with IRP.

The $o + s = p$ formula may help the teacher to create in her mind the necessary structure. The $O$ in the formula pertains to openness, the idea of personal involvement based on interest. $S$ stands for stability. Unless stability is maintained, productivity $(P)$ is reduced. Too many teachers have attempted IRP only to retreat because of the s in the formula. The purpose of this paper is to stress the s in the $o + s = p$ formula. For stability is the key to successful IRP. The structure in IRP is governed by this concept.

## Six Steps to Individualized Reading

Six identifiable steps to an individualized reading program, when followed successfully by the teacher, will lead to productive reading. Positive results are obtainable through IRP only when there is not too much stumbling on any of these steps. Teachers must understand each step and its relative importance to the total program of individualized reading.

The six steps are as follows:

1. Classroom environment—an atmosphere for productive reading.
2. Silent or quiet reading time—how to behave in reading class.
3. Instructional guidance—principle of noninterference.
4. Book talks and conference time—what should or should not be.
5. Skill development. USSR—the epitome of reading skills.
6. Records and evaluation—for benefit of learner.

The structure of IRP which the teacher must carry in her mind is derived from this framework. Proper development of this framework will prevent stumbling on the steps; teachers, thus, will avoid pitfalls in their efforts to build stronger classroom reading programs.

### The Reading Atmosphere Within the Classroom

The first step, which is basic to success, is to build a climate for productive reading. Building this atmosphere for reading takes careful nurturing and time. Each teacher's goal must be to develop productive silent reading on the part of each pupil. It is easy to make the mistake of leaving atmosphere to chance or of taking it for granted. Two key factors for creating this climate are the concept of quiet reading time and skillful use of instructional guidance.

*Quiet or Silent Reading Time*

The concept underlying silent reading time is vital to developing IRP successfully. Each teacher must clearly perceive legitimate activities for the silent reading period. The ideal model has each reader directing his own activities with printed material throughout the duration of the reading period. The perfect situation requires that everyone be so engaged in silent reading (or working on responses thereto) that the teacher is free to interact with pupils in a variety of ways, individually or in groups. It is helpful to have a chart visible to each reader and giving the framework or structure of the silent reading time. A sample chart could read as follows:

*Quiet Reading Time*

1. Select book or other printed material.
2. Read quietly (see how much you can get done).
3. Have a book talk or conference (be prepared—know what to say).
4. Record your results—write about reading, chart your progress.
5. Study vocabulary.
6. Work with a partner.

The behavior of the reader is markedly different in IRP from that which he has used in the text program. While natural for many, this new pattern is difficult for some. Pupil success in IRP requires the following:

1. Making wise and intelligent selections of reading material.
2. Spending large blocks of time in independent silent reading.
3. Preparing for and being ready to make the best contribution during the conference time.
4. Preparing reports, keeping records, and being ready to share learning from books with others.

Teachers err in not giving sufficient time and effort to establishing the framework for the quiet reading period. They frequently are too eager to move to conferences and book talks and leave the silent reading to care for itself. Moving too quickly to conference activities frequently does not work. Many young readers need constant instruction in sustained silent reading prior to gaining the self-direction needed to make conference time worthwhile. Initially some young readers need instructional guidance more than they need book talks.

## Instructional Guidance

Reading is not taken seriously by some pupils. Many boys and girls prefer to spend silent reading time in more noisy endeavors. The gossips, those who prefer talking to reading, are common. The wanderers, those active little individuals (mostly boys) who would rather walk around than read, need considerable attention. The wanderers usually spend excessive amounts of time searching for suitable reading material. When pressed to settle down to productive reading, many excuses are forthcoming for not doing so. "Squirrels" collect books as their animal counterparts do nuts; squirrels get new books each day but are too busy gathering them to take time to read them. For them, the reading time is unproductive. Productive reading is most difficult for the foregoing children. Typically about one-fourth of the total group exhibit such evasive behaviors. IRP cannot succeed unless the teacher first works at moderating, if not overcoming, disruptive behaviors by means of instructional guidance. And this point is precisely where many teachers fail.

The guiding principle, which should be held inviolate, is as follows: *during the reading period no one may act so as to interfere with the productive reading of another*. This rule means no interruption of one reader by another unless this interaction contributes in some way to the productivity of both. Much legitimate interaction may occur among various readers.

The principle of noninterference of others and high productivity by each must be firmly established. IRP cannot succeed without it. Yet the teacher who finds this precept violated no more than a dozen times a day should not be discouraged. The teacher can err only by not attending to the problems which arise and by not working to ameliorate them. Little by little the wanderers, gossips, and squirrels become readers. The basis for successful IRP has been established. Instructional guidance is crucial to creating the atmosphere of a successful quiet reading time. The rule of noninterference must work.

## Book Talks and Conferences

The silent reading time, with the atmosphere of productive reading created by it, is the heart of IRP. Similarly, conference time with book talks is the heart of the silent reading time. Through book talks the teacher plays a key instructional role, which must be clearly understood. In the past the role of the teacher in book talks has been poorly defined; consequently, serious mistakes have been made.

The first possible error is that teachers think the main purpose of book talks is to interrogate readers about each and every book read. The concept that extensive reading developed within IRP is exploratory in nature (i.e., searching far and wide in print of all sorts for important ideas) must be understood by both reader and teacher. Consequently, book talks should be based on sampling techniques. The teacher takes samples of each student's accumulated reading. Certain parts of some books are discussed, but not all parts of all books. Through conversation with readers, the teacher helps focus on key ideas that the readers have gained through a variety of situations. Thorough questioning of material read should be reserved for intensive reading which accompanies the textbook reading program and should not be duplicated in IRP.

Second, the conference time should not be used for checking oral reading errors. To think of the teacher's role as that of listening to individuals read orally is self-defeating for IRP. Again, this work can better be accomplished within the context of the textbook program with its oral reading groups.

The essential purpose of book time is to enable each reader to reveal the significance of his reading experience. The role of the teacher is to enable the reader to convey the true meaning for him of what has been read. The key to book talk time lies in the questioning used by the teacher. Perceptive, penetrating questions can give insight relatively quickly into the depth of reading.

## USSR: *The Pinnacle of Reading Skills*

Every teacher of reading should think of USSR as the pinnacle of achievement with regard to teaching skillful reading. In this instance the initials stand for uninterrupted sustained silent reading.

USSR pertains to the relativity among reading skills. Basic to the concept is the consideration that silent reading is far more significant than is oral reading, that contextual reading is of greater importance than are skills of recognition at the word/letter level, and that the greatest reading skill to be achieved is that of sustaining silent reading over long stretches of print without interruption and without breaks. USSR cannot be achieved unless the reader has the facility to keep his mind on and flowing with the ideas.

USSR, then, is the skill which signals that the student is able to read by himself and for himself over long spans of print. Each reader must realize that his purpose in the silent reading time is to get as many of the important and significant ideas as he can through silent reading. In USSR, reading is regarded as a detective-type activity, meaning that the reader is not held accountable for every single idea contained in every single sentence or parts thereof and that the reader is oriented to search the material for ideas which are of relatively great importance, i.e., ideas of relative importance as contrasted with detail and facts of lesser importance.

A radically different orientation to comprehension than that conveyed to the reader by the majority of current textbook programs is required. Both teacher and reader must understand that reading comprehension is making a series of judgments about the worthwhileness of the ideas, not remembering and repeating all that has been read.

USSR can be taught. Productive reading can be strengthened by helping each reader realize that success means learning to sustain himself with print for longer and longer periods of time. Any device the teacher uses to help the readers attain this goal is in order. Various instructional devices help youngsters keep track of the amount of silent reading accomplished during the reading period, i.e., through charts, graphs, or any scheme of time-keeping which will make progress visible. Another approach is for the teacher to sit with groups in the reading circle and supervise their silent reading. Here the teacher's role is simply to support and assist each youngster as he tries to get as far as he can with his printed material during his time in the reading circle. Oral reading is confined to having individual students verify ideas. The teacher helps with words; she assists in interpreting sentences; but more than anything else, she simply establishes the setting so that maximum amounts of silent reading can be completed by each child. The teacher helps each child to extend his own previous limits through day-to-day practice.

The USSR concept has significant implications for work with pupils at the lower end of the reading scale. A mistake has been made in attempting to teach the low group readers through oral reading. An erroneous practice has been the one of trying to get those in low groups to sound as good while reading orally as do those in upper groups. Attempting to reach relatively high degrees of oral reading fluency first is going at skill tasks backwards. Helping a young reader develop power of silent reading is the first priority. Teachers can develop silent readers first; fluency in oral reading will then follow naturally. More than anything else, priorities must be realigned with regard to basic reading skill areas.

## Record Keeping

Teachers using the individualized approach to reading instruction have devised ways for keeping records of the children's development in reading. Some find that a card or notebook page for each child can be easily used to record notes during the pupil conferences. Others use a more formalized checklist on which the teacher periodically records observations concerning the children's performances and abilities. Such records serve as a guide for planning and a basis for reporting to parents on the child's progress. If keeping records, keeping track of books, answering questions, or writing resumes on books read take more time, however, than is spent by readers reading, then the teacher has become lost in nonessentials.

*Evaluation*

Where the goal is that of developing independent readers, evaluation becomes a complex matter. The evaluator must know many aspects of each child's reading.

The teacher must know if the young reader performs effectively in the complex world of printed material. Does the reader find the sources important to him and then find the truly significant ideas within them? Most important, once the proper reading material has been selected, does the reader have the staying power to follow through on long intricate passages? Fortunately each student reveals the answer to these questions through his daily performance in IRP. Evaluation becomes a self-evaluation for many. Observant teachers can actually know each student's performance in reading better than in more conventional reading programs. It is a relatively easy matter for the experienced teacher to observe the relative ratio of talent and effort. It is the interaction of these two attributes which must ultimately form the basis of any meaningful evaluation.

Two major concepts are considered in this paper. First, a distinction is made between two forms which have resulted from the thrust toward individualized instruction in education. Prescriptive individualization associated with IPI is distinguished from a personal form of individual instruction found in the more typical individualized reading program (IRP). Features which differentiate the two forms of individualization are outlined, the structure which is usually highlighted as the contrasting factor between the two forms being challenged. The difference is not one of structure (prescribed) versus unstructure (personal) but rather one of the nature of structure. The personal component of IRP can be realized only through a rather delicate structure which rests in the mind of the teacher. The second major concept, a delineation of the structure needed to succeed in IRP, consumes the remainder of the paper.

# PART TWO

# Strategies for Improving Remedial Reading

GEORGE D. SPACHE
Jacksonville University

STRATEGIES FOR REMEDIAL READING or the treatment of learning disabilities may be categorized under three headings: those inherent in the direct pupil-teacher relationship; those involving a therapeutic or psychological approach; and those concerned with the academic progress of the learner. Each of these approaches makes certain assumptions about the learning process and employs techniques which appear consonant with those assumptions.

## Pupil-Teacher Relationship

*Question strategy.* Certainly the most basic of the pupil-teacher relationships is the question and answer pattern employed in the classroom. By the very nature of her questions, the teacher reveals her concept of the learning process and what she thinks is the best way of promoting the performances she desires. In the area of reading, the average primary teacher focuses two-thirds of her questions on the parrot-like recall of a line the child has just read. About 50 percent of the questions of intermediate grade teachers are also of this immediate recall type (2). Even when other types of thinking—such as evaluation—appear to be stressed, the expected answers are most often a simple "yes" or "no." Obviously the average teacher's concept is that learning is memorizing facts and reciting them.

*Cognitive development strategy.* In contrast to this extremely narrow view of learning there is the concept of reading as a thinking process. Cognitive development is the current term applied to the learning process, with the implication that various types of reasoning differ from child to child and that development of these processes can be stimulated. To illustrate, Clark's experiments (1) have tried to differentiate convergent and divergent thinkers in reading. Convergent readers are relatively slow, with good mastery of detail, but with poor comprehension of the total meaning or its implications. Divergent readers would be less dependent upon word recognition than context and show greater ability to deal with implications and inferences. Clark's tests seemed to bear out his dichotomy of interpretive, creative learners and detailistic, constricted learners. Other writers are exploring the differences between analytic-synthetic, objective-subjective, and field dependent-field independent or constricted vs. unconstricted learners. As yet, there has been little translation of these ideas into instructional practices. Teachers do not generally think of learning as training in reasoning processes. Perhaps we may look forward to the time when teachers realize that the questions they ask and the tasks they propose are really exercises in types of thinking. Perhaps teachers will realize that their true goal is stimulation of the child's thinking capacities, not his ability to recite facts exactly as he reads them.

*Grouping strategy.* The effects of classroom organization and classroom climate upon learning have been known for some time. We know, for example, that a group of people who succeed in a proposed task share certain characteristics: a common goal; a feeling of togetherness, an esprit or group identification; and an evolutionary process which brings forth leaders and followers. Yet, the strategy of small group instruction, as we see it in the classroom, violates all the principles of group dynamics. An authoritarian teacher constantly plans for her children and keeps them work oriented; as a result she incites hostility, aggressiveness among the members, and produces, at best, only temporary gains in pupil learning. Probably only children who are anxious or compulsive benefit from teacher-directed grouping and highly structured instruction. Spontaneous or flexible grouping based on children's common interests, which might breed self-reliance and initiative and perhaps produce permanent changes in attitudes toward learning, is seldom employed.

When children fail to learn in a highly structured basal reading program, or in a programed series, how many remedial teachers recognize the clue that a more individualistic approach might be more successful? Teachers in remedial reading and learning disabilities have not begun to look for the relationships among pupil personality, classroom organization, and teaching methods.

## Therapeutic Relationships

*Counseling strategy.* Some workers in reading and learning disabilities recognize that the child's difficulties may be a symptom of his faulty adjustment to school and life. Some recognize that failure to learn may be a revolt against parental pressure or sibling rivalry, or a means of perpetuating infancy, or an expression of defensiveness or hostility. With this point of view, improvement in learning is approached by techniques intended to improve the social and personal adjustment of the pupil. Marked gains in learning performances have been achieved by such treatments as play therapy, personal and group counseling, and parental counseling. Holliday (*3*), for example, used a combination of play therapy, group discussion, bibliotherapy, and creative writing with groups of normal and emotionally disturbed children. Reading gains were significantly greater for disturbed children given both remedial training and therapy. Adjusted children did not respond differently to remedial or combined therapies.

Recent studies have concentrated on increasing teachers' sensitivity to a pupil's self-concept and feelings about his capacities. Prows (*4*) found significant positive changes in pupil personality adjustment, self-concept, and breadth of reading when the teacher was trained in self-concept building and used an individualized approach. Like many earlier studies, these confirm the fact that for some types of children, the relief of a learning difficulty is best achieved by treatment of the child, not by treatment of his learning symptoms.

*Behavior analysis.* Psychological methods for treatment of the individual have recently been extended in two new approaches, behavior analysis and behavior modification. Detailed analysis of the desired learning behavior results in a programed, step-by-step sequence of tasks. By careful manipulation of stimulus, response, and reinforcement, the learner is led through a myriad of steps in acquiring the subskills which underlie a major performance. Close observation of the learning rates of a small number of pupils permits the refinement of the components of a program, which then may be used with many pupils. In fact, some authors of programed learning materials apparently feel that their sequences are suitable for all children. They maintain that this is individualized instruction since each child works alone with the workbook or the computer despite the fact that all the children pursue virtually the same learning steps.

*Behavior modification.* The logical extension of this Pavlovian manipulation of learning in small steps has appeared in what is called behavior modification. This is a system of rewards and punishments employed constantly to reinforce or extirpate pupil behavior. Each time a child succeeds in a task or exhibits a certain behavior, he is praised and given a tangible reward such as candy or plastic tokens. The tokens may be exchanged immediately or accumulated for a later treat, trip, or other privilege. Undesirable behavior is punished by fines exacted in the same medium. Behavior shaping has been found effective in remedial programs, particularly for lower-class children, as well as in treatment of the emotionally disturbed.

## Academic Strategies

*Skill development.* The visitor to a learning center is almost always impressed by the obvious emphasis upon skill development through the media of workbooks, charts, dittoed sheets, kits, readers, and audiovisual devices of many types. It is apparent that the primary strategy of the field is the repair of deficient skills. After all, aren't reading and spelling composed of many interdependent subskills? Doesn't it make sense to practice each of these skills separately in the hope they will blend together in the final performance? Unfortunately, this logic is not so sound as it appears.

Rather, we know that an eclectic approach employing several media of learning is not necessarily superior to instruction through the one medium through which the child might learn (if this medium is identified). Moreover, the importance or even the existence of many of the subskills we drill so intensively is not demonstrated. Instead, we know that all pupils do not employ the same skills in order to read successfully; for there are good readers who lack some skills, while some poor readers fail despite adequate performances in these same skills. To be specific, some children learn to read although they have very poor auditory discrimination; others having this ability may fail to learn. It is the opinion of the writer that many learning centers employ a scattergun approach, exposing the child to every device or method available in the hope that one of these will do the job. At the other end of this continuum of biased remediation, there are those centers that have a single, magic system applied to every child they treat. How much meaning does the term *diagnosis* have in these settings?

*Language development.* Research on preschool and economically deprived children has revealed that children lacking in experiences with language cannot readily succeed in school tasks. One strategy in answer to this cause of school failure has been the use of the language experience approach, basing initial reading on the actual language development of the child. The child learns to read his own ideas in his own vocabulary. As his store of ideas or words grows, so does his reading ability. Thus, reading, writing, and spelling are seen as part of his overall development in oral, written, and auditory language abilities. And, for many of these children, stimulation to language growth must be provided much earlier than the school years. Early language development may well become a significant preventive strategy of the future.

*Visual and motor training.* Another strategy for overcoming learning difficulties is manifested in the various visual and motor training programs. There is, of course, the creeping-crawling program sponsored by Delacato, a program refuted both by the research and competent medical authorities. But other training programs based upon optometric concepts of the interrelatedness of visuomotor skills and school achievement are appearing. Chalkboard and paper and pencil exercises, the walking beam and balance disc, templates, and classroom games are employed to improve ocular motility, orientation to directionality and space, and form perception. Among the research studies supporting this strategy is the first grade study of this author (5). In a year-long experiment, we found that visual motor training significantly contributed to the reading success of the economically deprived pupils and those in the lowest quarter of intelligence. Subsequent trials in two large school systems gave similar results, particularly when the training was combined with the language experience approach and a strong emphasis upon individualization of instruction.

*Summary.* Each of these strategies presupposes a somewhat different definition of learning. One, for example, assumes the task is recalling the exact facts offered in a book. Another assumes that children show varying reasoning abilities, and that our task is to stimulate these capacities. One strategy assumes that children learn best when the teacher is talking and directing them, not by efforts toward their own goals. Another approach suggests that learning difficulties are symptoms of the pupil's social and personal adjustment and that their correction lies in treating the child, not the apparent difficulty.

Still other strategy theories suggest that, as in laboratory animals, learning in children may be conditioned by controlling the conditions, the reinforcements, and the rewards. A very common theory emphasizes drilling in a host of separate little skills, one by one, until an amalgam of the polished performance appears. Finally, two recent strategies emphasize the need of intensive language development and visual motor training as preventive steps to avoid learning difficulties, particularly among children with poor academic prognosis.

## REFERENCES

1. Clark, Philip. "Reading Comprehension as Information Processing," *College and Adult Reading,* Third and Fourth Yearbooks of the North Central Reading Association, 1965, 96-105.
2. Guszak, Frank J. "Teacher Questioning and Reading," *Reading Teacher,* 21 (December 1967), 227-234.
3. Holliday, Kathleen Mahoney. "Values of Combined Remedial Reading Techniques and Certain Types of Psychotherapy for Emotionally Disturbed and Normal Pupils," doctoral dissertation, University of Florida, 1968.
4. Prows, Nancy Lejeune. "An Attempt to Increase Reading Achievement by Organizing Instruction and Sensitizing the Teacher to Building Positive Self-Concepts," doctoral dissertation, University of Florida, 1967.
5. Spache, George D., et al. *A Longitudinal First Grade Readiness Program,* Cooperative Research Project No. 2742. Florida State Department of Education, 1965.

# Pilot Study Using Selected Published Material for Retarded Readers in Secondary Social Studies

JAMES B. WILSON
East Texas State University

TEACHERS often complain that grade level material does not meet the needs of the retarded reader. Teachers may have the idea that they must follow a rigid, inflexible pattern as outlined in the state or local school district course of study. This idea tends to generate a precise and well-established pattern for the student as he progresses through the various grades in school. Teachers maintain that if they had materials that were appropriate for the retarded reader, these students would be able to perform satisfactorily in the classroom.

The purpose of this investigation was to determine the effectiveness of selected published materials that have been developed for the retarded reader. This investigation carried on in a metropolitan high school involved the introduction of new materials in American history, written especially for retarded readers.

## Method

One hundred and sixty-seven eleventh grade students were assigned to six American history classes by computer scheduling employing a random technique.

To identify students as retarded readers, the available records of students enrolled in the tenth grade during the previous school year were reviewed. In the identification of the students, the following sources of information were used: 1) scores on the California Test of Mental Maturity; 2) achievement scores on the Iowa Test of Educational Development, Tests I and V; 3) achievement scores on the Cooperative English Test, Form 1A; and 4) recommendations of teachers, counselors, or principals.

The following criteria were established for the initial selection of students for the classes for retarded readers: 1) intelligence quotient of 68-90, 2) achievement scores below the 34th percentile on the Iowa Test of Educational Development and the Cooperative English Test, and 3) staff recommendation.

Students selected for the pilot study were administered the California Test of Mental Maturity at the beginning of the investigation for the purpose of a double check on available information concerning intelligence. There was little difference between the available test scores and the scores on the California Test of Mental Maturity.

Achievement tests were administered at the beginning and the end of the study to determine progress as a result of the use of the new materials. Alternate forms of the following tests were administered:

1. Crary American History Tests, Forms E and F.
2. Metropolitan Achievement Tests, Forms Am and Bm.

Other tests administered included the unit tests which accompanied the selected materials.

## Treatment of the Data

The California Test of Mental Maturity was administered to check the accuracy of classification of students as retarded readers, based on the criteria used during the investigation (IQ of 90 or below). The results of this test are in Table 1.

*Metropolitan Achievement Test 1, Reading.* The results of the Metropolitan Reading Test, Forms Am and Bm are in Table 2. The raw score mean on the pretest was 15. The standard score which corresponds with the pretest mean was 39, according to the norms established for the reading test. The standard deviation on the pretest raw scores was 5.5. This indicates that approximately two-thirds of the scores were between a standard score of 28 and 49, or according to the norms for the test, between the 4th and 33rd percentile.

The raw score mean on the post test was 16.9. The standard

## TABLE 1

### RANGE OF INTELLIGENCE OF 167 STUDENTS

| Intelligence Quotient | Number of Students | Percentage of Students |
|:---:|:---:|:---:|
| 90-92 | 7 | 4.2 |
| 87-89 | 26 | 15.6 |
| 84-86 | 28 | 16.8 |
| 81-83 | 30 | 18.0 |
| 78-80 | 20 | 12.0 |
| 75-77 | 22 | 13.1 |
| 72-74 | 21 | 12.6 |
| 69-71 | 12 | 7.1 |
| 66-68 | 1 | .6 |

Mean ................................................... 83
Standard Deviation ..................................... 6

score which corresponds with the post test mean is 43, according to the norms established for the reading test. The increase in average standard scores between the pretest and post test was four standard score points. The standard deviation on the post test raw scores was 5.8, an increase over the pretest of .3 score points. Approximately two-thirds of the scores on the post test were between a standard score of 33 and 51, or, according to the norms for the test, between the 6th and 38th percentile.

The percentile standings on the Metropolitan Achievement Test 1, Reading, are in Table 3. Seventeen students scored above the 33rd percentile on the pretest, while 30 students reached above that

## TABLE 2

### SCORES ON METROPOLITAN ACHIEVEMENT TEST 1, READING FOR 167 STUDENTS

| Test Form | Raw Score Mean | S. D. | Standard Score High | Low |
|:---|:---:|:---:|:---:|:---:|
| Am—Pretest | 15.0 | 5.5 | 65 | 7 |
| Bm—Post Test | 16.9 | 5.8 | 69 | 7 |

TABLE 3

PERCENTILE RANK OF 167 STUDENTS ON METROPOLITAN
ACHIEVEMENT TEST 1, READING

| Test | Percentile Rank | | |
| Form | Above 33rd | 3rd-33rd | Below 3rd |
| --- | --- | --- | --- |
| Am—Pretest | 17 | 140 | 10 |
| Bm—Post Test | 30 | 126 | 11 |

same point on the post test. The ten students with a standard score of less than nine on the pretest also scored a standard score of less than nine on the post test. These students received intelligence scores between 68 and 71 on the California Test of Mental Maturity.

## Findings

The results of the standardized and unit tests administered during this investigation indicated the following:

1. According to the results of the Metropolitan Achievement Tests, the majority of the group showed little change between the pretests and the post tests. Some students showed an increase in reading, social studies skills, social studies vocabulary, and social studies information while some showed a decrease in these areas.

2. According to the results of the Crary American History Test, the majority of the group showed little change between the pretest and the post test.

3. According to the results of the unit tests for the selected published materials, most students showed satisfactory achievement. Based on a 100 percent scale, the mean performance for the group for the nine unit tests was 69.

This pilot study was undertaken from an observational approach and was effective in that it provided for an in-the-school observation and evaluation of the significant successes or lack of successes in meeting the instructional needs of the retarded readers in a school situation and for the reporting of the successes or failures in attempting to meet the instructional needs of retarded readers.

## Proposals

The following proposals are suggested for establishing programs for retarded readers: allocation of adequate time for planning a program, selection of teachers who are qualified and who will accept the challenge of working with retarded readers, provision for adequate inservice education for teachers of retarded readers, use of careful procedures in the identification of retarded readers, selection of materials to be used with retarded readers which provide for a wide range of individual differences within the slow learner group, selection of materials which contain a wide variety of suggested motivational techniques, selection of programs which agree with the school system's stated objectives, selection of careful procedures to study the behavior of students in a selected program, evaluation based on the individual student's achievement, placement of the emphasis in instruction on basic skills such as reading, placement of curricular emphasis on concrete experiences by use of community resources and audiovisual aids, and orientation of all staff members regarding programs for retarded readers.

## Conclusions

This development and implementation of a program for retarded readers using selected materials revealed a number of significant points. This pilot project seems to justify the following conclusions which have application to situations similar to those existing in this study.

1. Special materials designed for retarded readers do not influence the achievement of students as measured by group tests.

2. Students utilizing selected materials designed to increase reading level show a slight increase in reading ability as evaluated by group tests.

3. The students who received instruction using the selected materials remained approximately the same in social studies skills, social studies information, and social studies vocabulary as determined by group tests.

4. Behavior problems were not eliminated through the use of special materials and procedures in the classes for retarded readers.

## Implications

The following implications regarding the development and implementation of programs for retarded readers are presented as a result of this investigation:

1. The use of any selected materials for retarded readers will never release the teacher from his responsibility in the learning process. Selected materials should be used to supplement, rather than supplant, teaching procedures and materials.

2. In any learning situation, students progress at their own individual rates; thus, maximum learning cannot be expected from all students engaged in a program using selected materials because of the differences in motivation and study habits.

3. The use of selected materials designed for retarded readers is relatively new; teachers should have a thorough knowledge of the uses. Instructors who utilize the techniques suggested by authors of selected materials in their classrooms need additional training in evaluation of selected materials.

4. To assure the maximum effectiveness of selected materials, a fully developed curriculum scope and sequence should be required before special materials are selected or utilized.

5. The success of any program for retarded readers is dependent upon an understanding and acceptance of its purposes and objectives. Select materials designed for retarded readers will be only as effective as the attitudes of students, teachers, counselors, and administrators will permit.

6. The retarded reader needs to be allowed to progress at his individual rate of learning. Before selecting special materials, teachers should evaluate their provisions for individual differences.

7. Interaction between the teacher and students is important in obtaining an harmonious classroom atmosphere. Therefore, rapport may be more easily maintained in a group receiving a more individualized type of instruction than in a group receiving only the routine textbook instruction.

8. Group tests are used extensively in the public schools to determine achievement and intelligence standings. These tests are based on ability to read, and this ability or skill is a limitation to the rearded reader. More accurate testing of retarded readers could be accomplished, therefore, by the use of oral types of intelligence tests.

# Teenage Success: A Language Arts Program for the Nonacademic Student

LOUISE T. SCOTT
Florence, South Carolina, Public Schools

RESEARCH REVEALS a large number of poor readers in the secondary schools, a high relationship between dropouts and reading abilities, widely varying abilities within the classrooms, and an increasing lack of interest in reading among young people. The big question is "What can the secondary schools do to cope with these problems?"

In an attempt to answer this question, a description of the academic success enjoyed by nonacademic teenagers in a secondary language arts program follows. Nonacademic students are those who find academic achievement difficult and who are not primarily interested in furthering their education beyond high school.

## Recognition of the Need

As early as 1954 the school administration in Florence, South Carolina, public schools recognized the need for the teaching of reading beyond the elementary level and put into effect various procedures which did not produce the desired success. The results of 1967 random testing of the nonacademic students in grades seven through ten revealed a wide range of reading abilities within the classroom and emphasized the inadequacy of the existing English and reading programs.

## Organizational Procedures

*Preliminary planning.* The writer together with the state supervisors of English and reading, secondary principals, guidance counselors, reading teachers, and English teachers began formulating plans for a coordinated program of English and reading. Discussions at the first planning meetings centered around the need for developing a language arts curriculum based on levels of development rather than traditional grades. Appropriate instructional materials were previewed and evaluated. The extent of participation in each school was left to the discretion of the principal. Requests were received from five junior high schools for the establishment of 38 classes with 21 teachers.

One senior high school, which had expressed a serious concern about the inability of students to perform in the prescribed English curriculum, was selected for a special study.

*Organization of classes.* Based on results of reading survey tests administered in April 1968, the language arts program was organized on four phases of reading difficulty:

| *Phase* | *Reading Grade Level* |
|---|---|
| Phase I | R-3 |
| Phase II | 4-5 |
| Phase III | 5-6 |
| Phase IV | 6-7 |

Students comprising the four phases of the senior high level were divided by random sampling into experimental and control groups. Because of the wide diversity in reading abilities, students from grades ten, eleven, and twelve were grouped together in classes scheduled for two-period time blocks each day. Senior high students received one unit for English and one for remedial reading.

*Teacher selection and preparation.* Teachers were chosen because of their interest and desire to participate in the program. Formal educational qualifications for them included certification in English or, in grades seven and eight, certification in elementary education. Courses in reading were desirable.

Discussants at a five-day workshop in August included Harold Herber of Syracuse University and the state supervisors of English and reading. Teachers outlined the objectives and stressed the importance of teaching the students on their levels of achievement.

## Methods and Materials of Instruction

Psychological needs of teenagers such as realizing their worth as individuals, increasing self-confidence, experiencing success, and being accepted by peers were considered as well as academic needs. Classroom climate was such that most students experienced success and felt a sense of involvement in the total academic program rather than being designated as basic English students and remedial readers. Having a sense of belonging greatly improved attitudes. Since an informal atmosphere prevailed in classrooms, students felt free to express their thoughts in oral discussions and in writing. Criticism of oral expression and "red-marking" compositions were minimized.

Teaching the communication skills as components of the total language arts program instead of in isolation more firmly established the concept of language relationships. Listening, speaking, reading, and writing skills were closely coordinated to emphasize their interrelatedness to the total program.

*Developing listening skills.* Nonacademic students often have short attention spans, cannot follow directions, need increased skill in auditory discrimination, and have not developed various levels of listening ability. Opportunities were given students to hear, listen, and understand through class discussions, teachers' explanations, background music while they were writing, conversations, dramatizations, oral reports, records, phonic tapes, and oral reading by students and teachers. Other approaches placed emphasis on taking notes, playing listening games, completing listening exercises, and participating in all class activities.

Through listening activities, students with substandard dialects had opportunities to hear a standard dialect and develop sentence patterns acceptable to the community.

*Developing oral language skills.* In order for students to feel secure in expressing their thoughts orally, teachers accepted their dialects and oral language patterns. Some students needed to expand their own language and to see the importance of changing their speech patterns. The ability to use speech patterns appropriate to the locale, especially those patterns that bring about social acceptance, was a principal objective of the program.

In acquiring oral communication skills, teachers emphasized aural-oral approach with talking in personal conversations with peers and adults, telephone communications, class and group discussions, role playing, interviews, taped dialogues, retelling stories, choral reading, debating, dramatizing, and reading radio and television commercials. Students, grouped by pairing, practiced language development by using oral sentence patterns developed by teachers, oral language practice books, and oral reading to their partners.

The ability to communicate effectively was stimulated through the use of the tape recorder, video tape recorder, Language Master, telephone equipment on loan for class use, recorded speeches, oral language practice books, and a communication series.

*Developing skills for reading.* Reading deficiencies make some students potential dropouts. Insufficient reading skills, in the opinion of the content area teachers, seemed to be the basis of their problems. After students were placed into phases according to reading grade scores, teachers used informal inventories, check lists, and observations to determine individual needs. Instruction for students in small groups, in partnership study, in student-tutored groups, and in individualized study were forms of intraclass grouping used to meet these needs.

For some students, the goals of reading are those necessary for survival in society, such as reading newspapers; using telephone books; filling out forms; interpreting credit, savings, and interest rates; and understanding road maps and signs. Others need to become more proficient in word attack skills, to enlarge their vocabularies, to increase comprehension, to use study skills more effectively, to foster love for reading as a voluntary leisure-time activity, and to develop mature and refined reading tastes.

The reading program was divided into three areas, with each designed for a definite purpose. For the first area of developmental reading and literature, books and sets of paperbacks were selected by teachers, keeping in mind the interests of teenagers. Students shared experiences, discussed common stories, and achieved unity.

The second area was more individualized with each student being placed in material suited to his need and concentrating on building and reinforcing skills. Multiple skilltext on various levels of difficulty, skilltapes, word games, and multilevel labs were used to overcome problems in word analysis, vocabulary, comprehension, and study skills. Learning was made more interesting by the use of maps; periodicals; newspapers; forms, such as application, social security, insurance; brochures for military service; catalogs; telephone books; drivers' handbooks; savings account books; magazines; and records.

One of the most important areas is that of interesting teenagers in reading for pleasure. Approximately five thousand books, mostly paperbacks carefully selected on all reading and interest levels, were made available through classroom libraries. Many books were chosen from lists for bibliotherapy. Knowing that other people, although fictional, have been faced with similar problems helps teenagers solve their problems or to view them in a more favorable light.

*Developing composition skills.* As a departure from traditional methodology, the basic English text was replaced with a paperback text which coordinated the development of the four communication skills. Through practical application, the language principles taught inductively were used in composition exercises. Composition was made functional by integrating it with the reading selections. Rather than practicing by writing isolated sentences, students were asked to react to ideas basic to stories they had read.

The philosophy of learning to write through the practice of writing as advocated in *Hooked on Books* (1) was emphasized. Relaxed, unpressured writing activities as in journals give students opportunities to express their thoughts without fear of criticism. Pictures, paintings, recordings, films, filmstrips, transparencies, and personal experiences were used as stimuli for free-response writing. Expository efforts as writing a page on "How to Shine Your Shoes" or "How to Apply Makeup" were utilized as were several types of published materials. Pretending "If I Were," for instance a piece of chewing gum or a doormat, motivated some students to express their thoughts.

Teachers evaluated content as well as mechanics, concentrating on only one kind of error at the time. After reading compositions, teachers often discussed common errors and had students find their own errors. At the beginning of the year, some students were able to write only a few words or sentences, but later they wrote longer compositions with more clarity of expression.

*Operational guide.* As the program progressed, there was a need for the development of an operational guide to define more clearly the objectives and to coordinate the program of studies in the different phases. Guidelines set up included needs of the teenager, goals to be accomplished, skills to be developed, methods of instruction, materials, and kinds of evaluation. Such a guide helps teachers realize the importance of teenage needs, provides practical suggestions for effective instruction, and makes possible the exchange of ideas.

*Methods of reporting.* At the end of the first six-week reporting period, a letter explaining the program was sent to parents. Teachers commented on student progress. No student failed. A new language arts report card, omitting numerical grades and adding space for teachers' comments, was used.

Students progressed in basic materials at various rates, and different supplementary materials were used for different students. These factors necessitate students' progress cards which show the results of readying tests and English evaluations and progress in materials. Data are filed in cumulative records.

## Analysis of Data

Pretesting and post-testing on the vocabulary and comprehension sub tests of the *Gates-MacGinitie Reading Tests* were used to evaluate the effectiveness of the language arts program in the junior high schools. All schools made significant gains in comprehension as was determined by the use of $t$ tests. All but two schools made gains in vocabulary.

A nonstandardized English evaluation was used in pre- and post-testing to evaluate growth in grammatical usage, sentence identification, sentence arrangement, and sequential order in paragraphs. The $t$ statistics applied to data show significant gains made in sentence arrangement in all schools. Four schools gained significantly in sequential paragraph order; three, in sentence identification; and one, in grammatical usage.

The most noticeable improvement was shown in writing. A nonstandardized instrument was used in pre- and post-testing, and the data were statistically treated. All schools showed significant improvement in one or more of the following components: sentence sense, complexity of structure, surface conventions, vocabulary, frequency of stylistic devices, clarity of expression, and content.

To compare the new language arts curriculum with the traditional English instruction on the senior high level, experimental and control groups were established. Data were collected from pre- and post-testing, with the same instruments as used in the junior high schools and treated by means of a simple analysis of covariance. Neither group showed significant gain in vocabulary at any phase. In comprehension, the experimental groups showed gains at all phases, but the gains were significant only in Phases III and IV.

The greatest improvement in writing was shown in Phase I among the students who were in the readiness-to-grade-three levels in September and whose need to improve was the greatest.

## Concomitant Results

Although some teachers were doubtful about the length of the time block because of difficulty in interesting nonacademic students in formal grammar exercises and in literature with concepts they could not understand, the teachers within only a few months began to feel the period was too short. Students were not bored, and discipline problems were at a minimum.

After years of failure and frustration, many students experienced academic success. When one eighth grade boy received his report card, he jumped out of his desk and exclaimed, "I've been coming to school eight years and this is the first time I ever made a B!" Grading students on their own achievement made these grades possible.

Many students openly expressed their dislike for reading. After several weeks, classroom libraries afforded the most popular activity of the program. Students hid books so no one else could get "my book."

Consensus of the principals was that the program reduced the number of dropouts. Only one-fourth of the dropouts in the involved schools were in the program; three-fourths were in other English programs.

Dedicated teachers with deep understanding of human needs

have made the classrooms dramatic scenes of human development. Whereas the program did not provide solutions to all problems, the statistical data too strongly support its worth to be discounted; the enthusiasm of the faculty is proof that something of value has been accomplished; and the renewed faith of the teenage student that he can learn and that learning is fun is convincing evidence that this new language arts approach is far superior to the traditional program that has been used by the teaching profession.

REFERENCE

1.  Fader, Daniel N., and Elton McNeil. *Hooked on Books*. New York: Putnam, 1968.

# Reading Programs and Materials for the Educable Mentally Retarded

ALFRED L. LAZAR
California State College at Long Beach

HISTORY SHOWS that whenever teaching methods become inefficient, new methods are produced to meet the new conditions. The difficulties involved must first be clearly recognized before successful methods and techniques can be devised (*10*).

If those involved in special education programs for the educable mentally retarded would heed the foregoing observation, a more effective instructional program might be provided, especially in the area of reading. If the nature and degree of difficulties are to be minimized, several assumptions might be accepted as fundamental in developing effective and realistic reading programs for the educable mentally retarded. These critical assumptions are as follows:

1. that all methods and techniques are relative in time and space and are only a means to an end.
2. that the heterogeneous nature and range of abilities found in pupils identified and placed in special classes for the educable mentally retarded will necessitate an array of methods and techniques using a variety of materials.
3. that the teacher must realize that when progress is slow or ineffective the cause might not be centered in the child but rather in the teacher's failure to control and manipulate critical variables in the learning situation.
4. that the special class teacher be able to differentiate between individual attention and individualized instruction.
5. that the teacher assume the role as a manager of learning and approach education as a science rather than an art.
6. that the teacher develop a paradigm or model that would facilitate understanding, input, and control of various variables operating in the learning situation.

7. that feedback and various forms and kinds of evaluation are essential as part of a unified and systematic way for developing the reading curriculum and program.
8. that the teacher evolve a systems approach which will allow for scope and sequencing of knowledge, skills, and value development upon the part of both students and teacher.
9. that the teacher employ behavioral objectives as part of the daily learning plan.
10. that the special class teacher assume accountability for the production of learning as demonstrated by performance objectives.

The foregoing assumptions appear to be essential as part of the routine modus operandi of the scientific teacher and will be of even more significance with the growth in human knowledge in the years ahead, expanding technology, and mounting demand for teacher and administrator accountability as the cost of education increases.

### What Is Reading Behavior?

The purpose of this paper is to focus upon an operational definition of reading behavior, review selected literature on reading for the mentally retarded, and offer G-SOME System as a type of paradigm for use by the special class teacher in her reading program.

Reading behavior, according to Gibson (5) consists of a) receiving communication, b) making discriminative responses to graphic symbols, c) decoding graphic symbols into speech, and d) getting meaning from the printed page. The first requirement for learning this behavior sequence is the ability to talk and to understand the talk of others. The child must be able to speak and understand his own language in a fairly complex way and to use units of language organized in a hierarchy with a grammatical structure. After the child has achieved this mastery, he learns to discriminate the graphic symbols of his language and the spoken responses to graphic symbols.

Gibson has demonstrated that the reading process is exceedingly complex and requires the mastery of a series of skills, such as adequate reception, discrimination between sounds and symbols, visual and auditory input, sequence, and expression of ideas in the form of meaningful communication with significant others in the learning situation. Thus, the child first learns to read; afterwards, he reads to learn.

Many studies have been conducted concerning the mentally retarded and reading. Furthermore, the research has been grouped under various headings, such as reading capacity and achievement; comparative studies of the mentally retarded, normal, and gifted; mental age and beginning reading; and factors relating to the process of reading by the mentally retarded. Kirk (8) in his comprehensive review concluded with the following generalizations for each of the four areas.

## Reading Capacity and Achievement

In more than a dozen studies it was found that the mentally retarded in special classes read below mental age expectancy level, whereas in three studies it was found that the retarded group read at or above expectancy level. It was suggested that in cases where special attention is given to reading, reading ages might be expected to be in harmony with or slightly beyond the mental age.

## Comparison of Retarded, Normal, and Gifted Children

The conclusion cited in the previous section indicated that mentally retarded children in general read below their mental age reading grade expectancy. In contrast, we might ask whether normal or superior children read up to, beyond, or below their mental ages. The results of six studies indicated that when mental age is controlled, retarded children tend to be closer to their mental ages in reading than do superior children. Kirk (8) asserted that the retarded child who can learn to read is under pressure to achieve because, on the basis of his CA, he is retarded; whereas, the gifted child, in contrast, is not under the same pressure to achieve, since, on the basis of his CA, he is accelerated.

## Mental Age and Beginning Reading

A serious problem for some teachers at the primary level develops when they attempt to make a child with a CA of six begin reading while the child's MA might be five or four. Yet, if instruction in reading were delayed until children are six or six and one-half years of age mentally, they would be nine or ten years of age chronologically and would have been attending school from two to four years. Several studies concerned with preacademic programs found no significant differences between control and experimental groups.

## Rate of Progress in Reading

The studies on the rate of reading gain revealed conflicting findings. Dunn (4) concluded:

It is probable that under average conditions the increase in reading age parallels the increase in mental age. However, when the mentally retarded children who are reading considerably below their expectancy level are given intensive remedial instruction, gains may, at first, be quite rapid. This pattern probably ceases as reading age begins to exceed mental age.

## Goals at Various Levels

Kolstoe (9) outlines and identifies the following expected outcomes for reading at various school levels:

A. PREPRIMARY LEVEL:
  1. Has good skills of listening, such as auditory discrimination, memory, and closure.
  2. Has good skills of visual discrimination, memory, sequence, and closure.
  3. Recognizes meaningful configurations—i.e., signs STOP, WARNING, DANGER.
  4. Can read the letters of the alphabet.

B. PRIMARY LEVEL:
  1. Knows consonant sounds and blends.
  2. Knows vowel sounds.

   3. Knows beginning and ending sounds.
   4. Recognizes word families.
   5. "Reads" experience charts.
   6. "Reads" work sheets.

C. INTERMEDIATE LEVEL:
   1. Has a 220-word sight vocabulary.
   2. Uses phonics to attack new words.
   3. Uses context clues.
   4. Uses prefixes, suffixes, and root words.
   5. Can develop and read experience charts.
   6. Achieves a 2.5 grade level on reading achievement tests.
   7. Has an elementary grasp of newspaper readings.

D. PREVOCATIONAL LEVEL:
   1. Shows some interest in pleasure reading.
   2. Can read a newspaper to obtain information.
   3. Can develop and read detailed experience charts.
   4. Can use reading to get information.
   5. Understands and can use the dictionary.

E. VOCATIONAL LEVEL:
   1. Can read and understand crucial materials pertaining to bills and statements.
   2. Can read and understand simple sales contracts.
   3. Can read and use simple reference material.
   4. Enjoys human-interests magazines, i.e., Life and Look.

In contrast to the long list by Kolstoe, Smith (13) offers the following four specific objectives or goals:

A. Development of a basic sight vocabulary with elaboration on the existing speaking and listening vocabulary.

B. Development of a consistent method for word attack which is appropriate for each child and based on his idiosyncratic strengths and weaknesses.

C. Development of skill in and a desire to read independently for information, pleasure, and personal satisfaction.

D. Development of an adequate level of reading competence to allow for effective social and vocational participation in society.

These lists are presented for the reader's information and critical evaluation as to how valuable are they to a teacher. What is really needed for teacher usage would be a detailed taxonomy such as the one developed by Barrett for the cognitive and affective dimensions of reading comprehension (3).

## Viewpoints Past and Present

Johnson (7), after making a study of the various special class efficacy studies, concluded that mentally retarded children in special classes achieved significantly less than comparable children who remained in regular grades, despite small class enrollments, high educational costs, and specially trained teachers. He also concluded that any advantage in personal and social development which might be found in the special class groups appears "slight and probably not particularly meaningful." He attributed the negative findings of the efficacy studies primarily to teacher education programs which stress both the inability of the retarded and the need for establishing good mental health hygiene programs.

Blackman and Heintz (1) offer a different position:

> Research in the special education of the mentally retarded appears to be standing on the brink of a new era. The era we are about to leave is cluttered with the disappointments of studies that have attempted to demonstrate the value of special classes for the mentally retarded vis-a-vis regular class placement for these children. It is becoming more evident that profitable research in this area will take the form of developing and evaluating specific instructional systems which are derived from increasingly sophisticated psychological theory and to which the most appropriate components of an emerging educational technology have been applied. Special educators and educational psychologists will fulfill their promise to the mentally retarded when they begin to employ the rigor and controls currently at their disposal to achieve a better understanding of the psychological properties of school tasks as they interrelate with the abilities and disabilities of individual learners.

**Needed: A System for Organization and Function by the Special Class Teacher**

The rapid growth in educational technology and the vast sums of money being generated by both government and private industry in the areas of materials, diagnosis, learning research, and new training programs for young children, dropouts, and the handicapped create a serious problem for the individual special class teacher. Basically, this new difficulty or problem is how to assimilate and accommodate this rapid growth in knowledge, methods, and materials as part of one's teaching schema if these basic Piaget concepts are used. In addition, these growth phenomena offer the teacher the best opportunity yet for the individualization of instruction based upon the learning rate, interest, motivational, and modality input of each particular child.

Special education requires more than a tinkering job with the numerous fractional practices that are advocated by innovators of new methods, techniques, and materials, based upon limited or specific educational ends (11). To assist with this problem to some degree, Lazar (12) advocated the establishment of logistical control efforts for both teachers and administrators:

> It is no small wonder that we find teachers using materials and methods not of their own choosing, but which have been administratively imposed because of fiscal policies that influence the operation of the special classroom. One can imagine the emotional impact upon the teacher desiring some specific materials, say for reading, only to be told that she must wait until next year to put it on the requisition.
>
> If we expect the effective teachers in special education to provide realistic and individualized programs based upon prescriptive teaching approaches, efforts must be made to develop logistical guidelines for the procurement of materials when needed.

How are the growing problems in this area going to be resolved? The problem is to create unified systems that will facilitate communication, classification, and research and utilization of new methods and materials in a realistic, effective, and sane manner. It is time that systems be developed. The purpose of the system is realized through processes in which the interacting components of the system engage in order to produce a predetermined output. Purpose determines the process required, and the process will imply the kinds of components that make up the system. Thus, a system has three aspects (purpose, processes, and components) that furnish perspectives from which one can analyze and describe any existing system or use feedback to reconstruct a better one by changing the components (subsystems).

## G-SOME System for Reading Remediation

The purpose of the G-SOME System for reading remediation or instruction in reading per se is to provide the special class teacher with a logic system for planning educational objectives and making educational decisions. The G-SOME System is a logical model comprised of five major sequenced components that require the use of both vertical and horizontal feedback loops. Figure 1 provides an overview of the G-SOME System.

FIGURE 1. THE G-SOME SYSTEM COMPONENTS

| G ____ Variables | S Variables | O Variables | M Variables | E Variables |
|---|---|---|---|---|

Within each of the five major components are a series of variables that provide the need for task analysis action organization in helping the teacher make decisions in a scope and sequenced manner. The G-SOME System requires a thinking, creative teacher, one capable of making many critical decisions during a day's work. This view differs from educators who would reduce the teacher to being a doer-without-thinking because they would employ a prefabricated curriculum and minimize or reduce greatly teacher decision making.

A. *G Factors.* Eight factors or subsystems need to be considered by the new teacher during her initial planning and should be reviewed by the experienced teacher who already has an ongoing program and has completed her initial study of the eight factors. This component contains many significant social attitudes that can serve as intervening variables to influence the reading program and remediation effort. As it is well known, attitudes incorporate both feelings and beliefs and evaluation of objects and events on both an emotional and cognitive level. Knowledge of these factors not only offers the teacher a preventive program against taking actions and making decisions that would violate educational codes and policies but also offers ideas where influence and change need to be made in the program to gain community support.

FIGURE 2.   G VARIABLES. SOME CRITICAL FACTORS THAT INFLUENCE THE NA-
TURE AND THE DEGREE OF INSTRUCTIONAL EFFECTIVENESS AND PUPIL-TEACHER
INTERACTION DURING THE LEARNING SITUATION

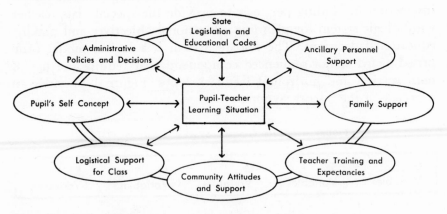

Reprinted with permission of Love Publications (see Reference *11*).

In Figure 3, a flow chart shows some 17 basic actions that might be taken by the teacher in developing a logic system for making educational plans and decisions when individualizing her reading program. Furthermore, it can serve as a method for the assimilation and accommodation of new ideas, materials, and theories into her teaching schema. The G-SOME System is a tentative model that can be adjusted and adapted to meet new requirements or the particular modus operandi of each teacher.

FIGURE 3. FLOW CHART OF THE SOME COMPONENTS REQUIRING CONTINU-
OUS TASK ANALYSIS ACTION UPON PART OF THE SPECIAL TEACHER

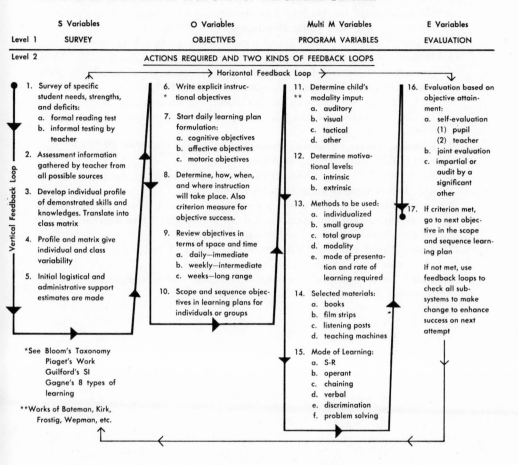

| S Variables | O Variables | Multi M Variables | E Variables |
|---|---|---|---|
| Level 1 SURVEY | OBJECTIVES | PROGRAM VARIABLES | EVALUATION |

Level 2 — ACTIONS REQUIRED AND TWO KINDS OF FEEDBACK LOOPS

→ Horizontal Feedback Loop →

Vertical Feedback Loop

1. Survey of specific student needs, strengths, and deficits:
   a. formal reading test
   b. informal testing by teacher
2. Assessment information gathered by teacher from all possible sources
3. Develop individual profile of demonstrated skills and knowledges. Translate into class matrix
4. Profile and matrix give individual and class variability
5. Initial logistical and administrative support estimates are made

*See Bloom's Taxonomy
Piaget's Work
Guilford's SI
Gagne's 8 types of learning

**Works of Bateman, Kirk, Frostig, Wepman, etc.

6.* Write explicit instruc- tional objectives
7. Start daily learning plan formulation:
   a. cognitive objectives
   b. affective objectives
   c. motoric objectives
8. Determine, how, when, and where instruction will take place. Also criterion measure for objective success.
9. Review objectives in terms of space and time
   a. daily—immediate
   b. weekly—intermediate
   c. weeks—long range
10. Scope and sequence objec- tives in learning plans for individuals or groups

11.** Determine child's modality imput:
   a. auditory
   b. visual
   c. tactical
   d. other
12. Determine motiva- tional levels:
   a. intrinsic
   b. extrinsic
13. Methods to be used:
   a. individualized
   b. small group
   c. total group
   d. modality
   e. mode of presenta- tion and rate of learning required
14. Selected materials:
   a. books
   b. film strips
   c. listening posts
   d. teaching machines
15. Mode of Learning:
   a. S-R
   b. operant
   c. chaining
   d. verbal
   e. discrimination
   f. problem solving

16. Evaluation based on objective attain- ment:
   a. self-evaluation
      (1) pupil
      (2) teacher
   b. joint evaluation
   c. impartial or audit by a significant other
17. If criterion met, go to next objec- tive in the scope and sequence learn- ing plan

   If not met, use feedback loops to check all sub- systems to make change to enhance success on next attempt

REFERENCES AND NOTES

1. Blackman, L. S., and Heintz, P. "The Mentally Retarded," *Review of Educational Research,* 36 (1966), 15-16.
2. Bontrager, Ray. Concept of "Verbal Pollution" is Ray's idea, personal communication 1970.
3. Clymer, Theodore. "What Is Reading? Some Current Concepts," in H. M. Robinson (Ed.), *Innovation and Change in Reading Instruction,* Part II, NSSE Yearbook, 1968, 7-29.

4. Dunn, F. A. "A Comparison of the Reading Processes of Mentally Retarded Boys of the Same Mental Age," in L. M. Dunn and R. J. Capobianco, *Studies in Reading and Arithmetic in Mentally Retarded Boys.* Monograph Soc. Res. Child Development, 19 (1954), 7-99.

5. Gibson, Eleanor J. "Learning to Read," *Science,* 148 (1965), 1066-1072.

6. Hunter, M. "Individualizing Instruction," *Instructor* (March 1970), 53-64.

7. Johnson, O. "Special Education for the Mentally Handicapped—A Paradox," *Exceptional Children,* 29 (October 1962), 62-69.

8. Kirk, Samuel A. "Research in Education," in Stevens and Hebers (Eds.), *Mental Retardation.* Chicago, Illinois: University of Chicago Press, 1964, 57-99.

9. Kolestoe, Oliver. *Teaching Educable Mentally Retarded Children.* New York: Holt, Rinehart and Winston, 1970.

10. Korzbyski, Alfred. *Selections from Science and Sanity.* Lakeville, Connecticut: Institute for General Semantics, 1948.

11. Lazar, Alfred L. "The SOME Systems Approach: A Paradigm for Educational Instruction and Remediation by the Special Class Teacher," *Focus on Exceptional Children,* 1 (December 1969), 1-8.

12. Lazar, Alfred L. "Logistical Control in Special Education," *The Pointer,* 13 (Spring 1969), 49-52.

13. Smith, Robert. *Clinical Teaching: Methods of Instruction for the Mentally Retarded.* New York: McGraw-Hill, 1968.

# Learning of Basal Reading Skills by Mentally and Nonmentally Handicapped Children

IRA E. AARON
University of Georgia

THIS STUDY investigated intellectually retarded, normal, and superior pupils' achievement in basal reading skills over a seven-month instructional period. The investigation included the following five facets:

1. A comparison of retarded and normal groups' level and rate of acquisition in basal reading skills.
2. A comparison of intellectually normal and superior groups' level and rate of acquisition in basal reading skills.
3. The identification of sequences among basal reading skills and a comparison of the logically identified sequences with pupils' skills knowledge.
4. The examination of intellectual processes related to achievement in basal reading skills.
5. The description of trends in basal reading skills achievement over reading instructional levels 2, 3, 4, and 5.

Only the first two facets will be discussed here. Detailed information on all five parts can be found in *Learning of Basal Reading Skills by Mentally Handicapped and Non-Mentally Handicapped Children,* by Kathryn A. Blake, et al. The original study was supported by a grant from the Office of Education, U.S. Department of Health, Education, and Welfare (Project No. 5-0391, Grant No. 32-20-0450-1032). The report is deposited with ERIC (ED No. 014406).

## Basal Reading Skills and Intellectual Processes Investigated

Fifty basal reading skills, falling in six skills categories, were selected for investigation. One skill was classified as identifying words at sight; nine were classified as phonetic analysis skills; seven, as structural analysis; ten, as dictionary; eight, as word functions; and fifteen, as comprehension skills. Specific listings in each of the six categories will be presented in the discussion of the results.

Prior to the selection of the skills to be studied, currently used basal reading materials were examined and information was obtained about materials being used in school systems from which the sample was to be drawn. On the basis of these investigations, the Scott, Foresman *New Basic Readers* series was chosen. Skills were selected after a task analysis of the Scott, Foresman program from preprimer through reading instructional level six. The 50 skills selected were representative of important components of the reading act.

Tests were developed by the researchers to assess the 50 skills to be studied. These instruments were pilot tested and then revised. Subtests assessing knowledge of skills ranged from 6 to 48 items, with most subtests containing 12 or more items. Items, prepared mainly in terms of operational definitions, were based upon the task analysis of the Scott, Foresman program. Reliabilities for the various subtests ranged from a low of .42 to a high of .96, with a median of .76. Reliabilities were established by means of the split-half method and corrected by the Spearman-Brown Prophecy Formula.

## Subjects

Subjects were enrolled in 44 classes of grades two through five or special classes for the mentally retarded. Classes were selected from three Georgia school districts: one in a large urban area, a second in a middle-size urban area, and the third in a rural-small urban area. Criteria for subject selection were intelligence quotients of 50 or higher on the Stanford-Binet Intelligence Scale; fall placement at reading instructional levels two, three, four, or five in Scott, Foresman materials, as determined by an informal reading inventory; and adequate physical, sensory, and emotional development for response to the instructional program.

The intellectually retarded, normal, and superior groups consisted of a total of 308 pupils, 108 each in the retarded and normal groups and 92 in the superior group. Subjects in the retarded group ranged in IQ from 50 to 80; those in the normal group, from 90 to 110; and those in the superior group, 120 and upward.

## Procedures of the Study

The study covered a three-year period. The first year was devoted to selection of skills to be investigated, to preparation of testing instruments to be utilized, and to organizing the various logistical aspects of the project. During the second year, the investigation was undertaken. The final year was spent in data treatment and analysis and in preparing the final report. This section of the report will discuss activities of the second year of the investigation.

Subtests assessing 41 of the 50 basal reading skills were administered by classroom teachers during the first week in October and again during the first week in May. Directions for these tests were presented on tape to assure uniformity of administration. Five testing sessions were necessary for each administration of these tests. Tests assessing achievement on eight figurative language and critical reading skills were administered in late March and early April. Teachers also administered these tests, this time in three testing sessions. An individual sight vocabulary test was administered in September and October by project personnel.

This investigation, in part, involved comparing reading achievement of retarded and normal subjects and of normal and superior subjects who had been taught reading on corresponding instructional levels. Therefore, for valid comparisons, reading programs of pupils in the study had to be similar, insofar as such similarity is possible and warranted in regular school settings. In an effort to achieve the desired degree of standardization within each level of reading instruction, project directors furnished teachers with Scott, Foresman texts and accompanying materials and gave them general guides for instruction. Eight inservice sessions, beginning in early September and scheduled monthly thereafter, were held for teachers. All were asked to follow the general project instructional guides and the Scott, Foresman guidebook lesson plans. However, teachers were requested to vary rate of coverage of materials in terms of pupil needs. As in regular classroom use of a basal series, project teachers supplemented the program with additional materials.

## Results of the Investigation

A summary of the results of the two selected phases of the study is presented in the table at the end of the chapter.

### Retarded and Normal Groups' Achievement

One facet of the investigation compared the retarded and normal groups on level and rate of acquisition in basal reading skills. Retarded and normal groups had been equated on mental age and on general reading achievement level. Reading instructional levels two and three were combined into primary level and levels four and five into intermediate level.

For primary and intermediate levels treated separately, $t$ tests were used to determine the significance of the normal and retarded groups' level of acquisition on each basal reading skill at the beginning of the study. As the summary table shows, at the primary level, the normal and retarded groups' levels of acquisition were not different on 38 skills; the normal group exceeded the retarded group on 9 skills; and in one instance, the retarded group exceeded the normal group.

The second part of this facet dealt with rate of acquisition over the seven-month instructional period. A two-factor analysis of variance model was used to process the data. Fall and spring test scores, on those tests administered twice, and intelligence test results were used in the data treatment. At the primary level, the normal and retarded groups did not differ significantly on rate of acquisition of 21 skills, whereas the normal group's rate of acquisition exceeded that of the retarded group on 18 skills. The normal and retarded groups at the intermediate level did not differ significantly on rate of acquisition of 27 skills, but the normal group's rate of acquisition exceeded that of the retarded group on nine skills.

*Superior and Normal Groups' Achievement*

Another facet of the study compared the superior and normal groups on level and rate of acquisition in basal reading skills. Normal and superior groups were equated on chronological age. As in the case of retarded and normal group comparisons, primary and intermediate levels were treated separately; fall tests were used in studying levels of acquisition; fall and spring test results were used in investigating rates of acquisition; *t* tests were used to test differences in levels of acquisition; and a two-factor analysis of variance model was used in studying differences in rate of acquisition.

At the primary level, levels of acquisition for the superior and normal groups did not differ significantly on 17 skills; however, in 30 instances the superior group was superior to the normal group, and on one skill, the normal group's level of acquisition was significantly higher than that of the superior group. Superior and normal groups at the intermediate levels were equal in level of acquisition on nine skills; the groups differed significantly on 41, with the superior group showing the higher levels in all instances.

Rate of acquisition over the seven-month instructional period differed little at both primary and intermediate levels. On 29 skills at the primary level and 32 at the intermediate level, the two groups did not differ significantly in rate of acquisition. In seven instances at the primary level and two at the intermediate, the superior group's rate of acquisition exceeded that of the normal group; in one case at the primary level and two at the intermediate, the normal group's rate of acquisition was greater than that of the superior group.

## Implications

Among the implications that may be drawn from findings of this investigation are these:

1. Mentally retarded children *can* learn the skills of reading. At the primary level, the mentally retarded group compared favorably with the normal group on 39 of 48 skills. At the

intermediate level, the retarded group compared favorably with the normal group on only 22 of 50 skills.

2. Pupils, especially the superior pupils, should be taught the skills at earlier ages.
3. Teachers should expect pupils to achieve at higher levels.
4. Teachers should differentiate methods and materials in a way appropriate for the pupils' particular learning and motivational characteristics.
5. Secondary programs for mentally retarded students should give more attention to developmental reading.
6. Programs such as the one used in this investigation appear to be better suited to normal than to retarded and superior students.

## Limitations

An investigation of this nature has a number of limitations, and these must be kept in mind as generalizations are made. Some of the more important are these:

1. Generalizations must be limited to populations similar to the one from which subjects in this study were drawn.
2. Generalizations must also be limited to subjects in reading instructional programs similar to the program used in this study.
3. The investigation was limited to selected reading skills.
4. Behaviors pertinent to acquisition rate were based on only two assessments, seven months apart.

SUMMARY TABLE

| Skills Category | Skills | Retarded & Normal Groups | | | | Superior & Normal Groups | | | |
|---|---|---|---|---|---|---|---|---|---|
| | | Acq. Level | | Acq. Rate | | Acq. Level | | Acq. Rate | |
| | | Prim. | Int. | Prim. | Int. | Prim. | Int. | Prim. | Int. |
| Identifying words at sight | Identifying words at sight | * | * | — | — | S | S | — | — |
| Phonetic analysis skills | Assoc. vowel letters & sounds | * | * | * | * | * | * | — | — |
| | Assoc. consonant letters & sounds | * | * | * | * | S | * | * | * |
| | Assoc. consonant digraphs & sounds | * | * | * | * | S | S | N | * |
| | Assoc. consonant blends and sounds | * | N | * | * | S | * | * | * |
| | Ident. syllables in oral. & vis. presented short words | * | N | * | * | S | S | * | — |
| | Ident. syllables in vis. presented short words | * | N | * | * | * | S | * | * |
| | Ident. syllables in oral. & vis. presented long words | N | N | * | * | S | S | * | * |
| | Ident. syllables in vis. presented long words | N | N | * | * | * | S | S | * |
| | Using spelling patterns | N | N | N | * | S | S | * | * |
| Structural analysis skills | Ident. components of compounds | * | * | N | N | S | S | N | — |
| | Ident. roots, endings, & suffixes | * | * | * | N | * | S | * | * |
| | Ident. roots & prefixes | * | N | N | * | S | S | * | * |
| | Ident. roots & multiple affixes | * | N | N | * | * | * | N | * |
| | Locating roots by using root-change rules | * | N | N | * | * | * | * | N |
| | Changing roots by using root-change rules | * | N | N | * | * | S | * | * |
| | Translating contractions | * | N | N | * | S | S | N | * |

SUMMARY TABLE (*Continued*)

| Skills Category | Skills | Retarded & Normal Groups | | | | Superior & Normal Groups | | | |
|---|---|---|---|---|---|---|---|---|---|
| | | Acq. Level | | Acq. Rate | | Acq. Level | | Acq. Rate | |
| | | Prim. | Int. | Prim. | Int. | Prim. | Int. | Prim. | Int. |
| Dictionary skills | Ident. alphabetical seq. based on 1st letter | * | N | * | — | S | S | — | — |
| | Ident. alphabetical seq. based on 3rd letter | * | N | N | * | S | S | * | N |
| | Ident. alphabetical seq. based on 1st, 2nd, 3rd letter | * | * | * | N | * | S | S | * |
| | Using dict. guide words | * | N | * | * | * | S | * | * |
| | Finding definitions of single entry words | * | N | * | * | S | * | * | * |
| | Finding definitions of multiple entry words | * | N | * | N | S | * | * | * |
| | Selecting definitions of single entry words | — | * | — | * | — | S | — | * |
| | Selecting definitions of multiple entry words | — | N | — | N | — | S | — | * |
| | Interpreting single pron. symbols | * | N | N | * | S | S | * | * |
| | Interpreting multiple pron. symbols | R | * | N | — | * | * | * | S |
| Word functions skills | Recog. func. of nouns | * | * | N | * | S | S | * | * |
| | Recog. func. of verbs | * | * | N | N | S | S | * | * |
| | Recog. func. of adj. | * | * | N | N | S | S | * | * |
| | Recog. func. of adv. | * | * | * | N | S | S | * | * |
| | Spec. func. of nouns | * | * | * | * | * | S | * | * |
| | Spec. func. of verbs | * | * | * | — | * | S | S | * |
| | Spec. func. of adj. | * | * | * | * | * | S | S | * |
| | Spec. func. of adv. | * | * | * | — | N | S | * | S |
| Comprehension skills (Directly stated) | Ident. cause-effect rel. in sent. (dir. stated) | * | * | N | — | * | S | * | — |
| | Ident. details in stories (dir. stated) | * | N | N | * | S | S | * | * |
| | Ident. main ideas in paragraphs (dir. stated) | * | N | N | * | S | S | * | * |
| | Ident. main ideas in stories (dir. stated) | * | N | * | * | S | S | * | * |

SUMMARY TABLE (*Continued*)

| Skills Category | Skills | Retarded & Normal Groups | | | | Superior & Normal Groups | | | |
| | | Acq. Level | | Acq. Rate | | Acq. Level | | Acq. Rate | |
| | | Prim. | Int. | Prim. | Int. | Prim. | Int. | Prim. | Int. |
|---|---|---|---|---|---|---|---|---|---|
| Comprehension skills (Implied) | Ident. cause-effect rel. in sent. (implied) | * | N | * | * | S | S | * | * |
| | Ident. main ideas in paragraphs (implied) | * | N | N | * | S | S | * | * |
| | Ident. main ideas in stories (implied) | * | * | N | N | S | S | * | * |
| Comprehension skills (Others) | Inter. similes | N | N | — | — | * | * | — | — |
| | Inter. idioms | N | N | — | — | S | S | — | — |
| | Inter. hyperboles | N | N | — | — | * | S | — | — |
| | Inter. personification | N | N | — | — | * | S | — | — |
| | Inter. metaphors | N | * | — | — | S | S | — | — |
| | Predicting outcomes & actions | * | * | — | — | S | S | — | — |
| | Discriminating between fact & fiction | * | * | — | — | S | S | — | — |
| | Discriminating between fact & opinion | N | N | — | — | S | S | — | — |

* indicates two groups equal
— indicates no test made
N indicates Normal group exceeding
R indicates Retarded group exceeding
S indicates Superior group exceeding

# Reading Program for the Afro-American

ANTOINETTE C. DAVINO
Compton, California, City Schools

IN EVERY ETHNIC GROUP a unification of culture occurs by such labels as Afro-American, Mexican-American, Italian-American, French-American, or French-Canadian. These terms state that the person is a combination of both heritages or cultures, the prefix explaining his original heritage and background and the final term explaining his acquired heritage and social environment.

Culture is the sum of ways of living established by a group of human beings and transmitted from one generation to another. At the present time ethnic groups composed of dual cultures are experiencing cultural change, the process by which a culture is significantly modified for one or more various reasons.

Acculturation, or the process of culture change that takes place when people live in long, continuing contact with others, is more complex than the simple diffusion of traits. When two societies are in contact with one another, one does not completely abandon its former culture and completely accept the other's. An interchange of ideas and culture elements takes place. This is not an even process, and the rate and direction of change are dependent upon many factors (5).

It appears that the individual most affected by a dual culture is the school-age child, who lives in both cultures. He experiences in his home environment the customs and values of his parents and their heritage and in his school environment, the customs and values of the dominant influence in the society in which he is presently living. Difficulty arises for the child when the values and expectations of both cultures are so divergent that he cannot successfully operate in both of them (7).

When the dual culture child comes to school, he comes with something most important, a self and a sense of belonging to whatever group is his (2).

94

But how is "his group" determined? Each of the subcultures in America today has unique characteristics. Each also has similarities which are more the result of economics than heritage (1):

> Many of the ecological features of the segregated Negro subculture that impinge on personality development in early childhood are not specific to Negroes as such, but are characteristic of most lower-class populations. This fact is not widely appreciated by White Americans and hence contributes to much anti-Negro sentiment: many characteristic facets of the Negro's value system and behavior pattern are falsely attributed to his racial membership, whereas they really reflect his predominant membership in the lower social class.

Ever since Francis Galton in 1869 published his studies of hereditary genius, and perhaps long before, the existence of a substantial positive correlation between socioeconomic status and competence has been abundantly clear. Evidence continuing to affirm this association has continued to accumulate (6).

Social conditions cannot be ignored in education. Cohen (3), however, states:

> It appears that the school has served the useful purpose of relieving other social institutions of responsibility. If highway accidents increase, the school's driver education program is criticized. A Russian spaceship is launched, and the school science program is attacked. Venereal disease rates rise and the school must assume responsibility for sex education. Social immorality breeds segregated societies and the schools are again the scapegoat.
>
> The tragedy of the situation is that, while the school continues to accept the responsibilities of other social institutions, many educators are no longer clear about the nature of the function of their own institution. For example, when the black community cries out about the low reading achievement of its children, the school refuses to accept the responsibility. Instead, educators respond with long dissertations on the psychosocial factors of home, community, family structure, and so on, as determinants of low reading achievement. How ironic, indeed; for finally taken a stand, they stand the wrong way on the most crucial school issue—literacy.

Cohen's statement has many implications for educators. In some ways he is right. The school has assumed many of society's burdens. But in some ways he is wrong. The school cannot negate the psychosocial aspects of the child's home, community, and family structure. But the school, now realizing the background and environment of its students, can adjust to meet their needs.

According to Cohen the breakthrough in the teaching of reading to disadvantaged children will come if we concentrate on the methodology of teaching, rather than on the causes of the disadvantaged position. His reasoning is that the school is severely limited in any attempt to directly influence these factors. Nothing in the child's background automatically precludes his learning to read. The best method of promoting such achievement may derive from general laws of learning, not from the knowledge of his environment (3).

Again Cohen has a good point. General laws of learning should be applied; but they can better be applied with a knowledge of the child's environment. In the combination of these, not the exclusion of either, lies the answer to the teaching of reading to the disadvantaged.

During the first years of Operation Head Start differences in learned factors of readiness were observed among disadvantaged children. These differences were due to a lack of opportunity to learn as determined by the knowledge of the home conditions. From this knowledge, the school should realize that for children from homes where reading readiness is not taught incidentally, the school must teach it purposefully (3):

> Intensive, thorough instruction that meets individual needs teaches disadvantaged children to read adequately. Such instruction appears to counterbalance the effects of environmental deprivation when we use reading achievement scores as criterion for growth.

The tradition of purchasing one class a set program with its teacher's manual and a few supplementary storybooks is no longer valid. The practice does not provide an adequate reading program. Instead, teachers should select varieties of materials, programs, and pieces of programs to teach the developmental reading skills and then integrate these into skill sequences and dispense them according to individually diagnosed needs.

The foregoing implies that the teacher would have the necessary knowledge of the order and difficulty levels of the developmental reading skills. The teacher should also understand that reading is a process, not a subject, and should be taught accordingly and also that this process is developmental and sequential and should be taught in this way. Each part or skill should be mastered before proceeding to the next skill.

It cannot be assumed that a skill is learned in the first presentation. It should be taught, practiced, evaluated, retaught, and repracticed.

The most important area of practice is where the need for a variety of materials is evident. For some pupils no one program gives enough reenforcement for every skill. But if materials are used to complement and supplement, enough practice for each skill can be readily available. Instead of 32 workbooks from one company, four books from eight different companies can be much more effective, especially if the contents are cut up and categorized according to specific skills. Teachers can prepare individualized learning kits by clearly writing the directions, pasting the pages to cards, typing the answers on the back, and assigning the children the skill area in which they need practice. In this manner the activity becomes self-directing and self-correcting and meets the needs of the children much more effectively than one book can.

There are also many commercially prepared skills kits that can be adapted to meet the needs of a particular classroom.

Which one is the most effective in the classroom? Not any one—each has its strengths and weaknesses. Each has its place in the classroom, but not each alone. A variety is most effective when it is used in the classroom by a knowledgeable teacher who uses the strengths of the materials in an intensive instructional program that meets the individual needs of the students.

In every classroom there is a reading triangle, comprised of the teacher, the children, and the materials or the tasks to be learned. No matter how much we theorize and talk about methods, pedagogies, family structure, and all the other factors related to reading, we must return to the classroom triangle. It is the interaction and relationship between teacher, children, and materials that make a reading program. A serious deficiency in any of these three components can be the cause of reading failure, or a lesser deficiency in two components, or a mediocre deficiency in all three components.

According to Goldberg (4), it has become a cliché to state that the major effect on a child's learning results from what goes on in the classroom. We recognize that what the teacher and the children do during the time they are in direct contact with one another is the "compass of learning." And yet, until recently, little research has been aimed at the teaching process. We still cannot describe with accuracy what teaching is about, what the teacher actually says and does in the process of teaching, and what effect this instruction has on the child learning.

We also don't know why some teachers can be successful with certain materials and methods and other teachers need different materials and methods to be successful.

Goldberg (4) has set up a hypothetical model of the successful teacher of the disadvantaged. The successful teacher respects his pupils, views the culture of his pupils as a student, understands the backgrounds from which the children come, and recognizes and understands their unwillingness to strive for future goals where such efforts provide little reward in the present.

The successful teacher is aware of the ethnic group membership of his pupils and how this shapes the child's image of himself and his world. This teacher knows that the language of his pupils is closely tied to the lives they lead. Even though it may not be standard English, he recognizes its functional qualities for the child.

The teacher develops in his pupils certain key concepts of language (9). One important concept is the variety of language systems in our society; each can be identified and each is appropriate for the speaker who uses it. The language system that communicates ideas and feeling effectively and is comfortable for the speaker and listener is appropriate. A second key concept of language is that standard English is the variety of English understood by most people regardless of the particular varieties of English they themselves speak. Standard English is a kind of universal dialect in our society.

It is the variety of English used in many of the important affairs of society. Therefore, standard English must be learned as an alternate dialect. It must be mastered to the extent necessary to assure effective communication without embarrassment or discomfort. The pupil must understand in which situations standard English is appropriate. Further, students should understand the social, vocational, and academic benefits of learning and using standard English effectively.

In addition to his knowledge about the child in his environment, the successful teacher has an understanding of how a child's abilities are assessed and a realistic perception of what these measurements describe and predict. He knows that in the area of reading he must correctly diagnose the child's strengths and weaknesses and proceed to teach accordingly. The successful teacher meets the child on equal terms, as person to person. But, while the teacher accepts, he doesn't condone.

He realizes the danger of the "self-fulfilling prophecy" of expecting and, consequently, finding a low level of achievement. He, therefore, lets each pupil know that more is expected than the pupil thinks he can produce—but the teacher's standards are not so high as to become too remote to strive toward. He rewards, is alert to every opportunity for honest praise, and as much as possible withholds harsh criticism. But above all, he is honest.

This is the reading program for the Afro-American—a composite of the strengths of various programs adjusted to meet the needs of the individual students by a knowledgeable, caring teacher.

REFERENCES

1. Ausubel, David P., and Pearl Ausubel. "Research on Ego Development Among Segregated Negro Children: Implications for Education," Bureau of Educational Research, University of Illinois, 1962.
2. Calitri, Charles J. Improving English Skills of Culturally Different Youth in Large Cities. Washington, D.C.: United States Department of Health, Education and Welfare, Office of Education, 1964.
3. Cohen, S. Alan. Teach Them All to Read. New York: Random House, 1969.
4. Frost, Joe L., and Glenn R. Hawkes (Eds.). The Disadvantaged Child: Issues and Innovations. Boston: Houghton Mifflin, 1966.
5. Fuchs, Estelle. Teachers Talk. Garden City, New York: Doubleday, 1969.

6.  Hunt, J. McVicker. *The Challenge of Incompetence and Poverty*. Urbana: University of Illinois Press, 1969.

7.  Keller, Suzanne. "The Social World of the Urban Slum Child: Some Early Findings," *American Journal of Orthopsychiatry*, 33 (October 1963), 823-831.

8.  Passow, A. Harry, et al. *Education of the Disadvantaged*. New York: Basic Books, 1967.

9.  Sherk, John F., Jr. "Dialect—The Invisible Barrier," *Reading Bulletin No. 131*. Boston: Allyn and Bacon, 1969.

# Components of a Reading Program for the Mexican-American Child

RICHARD D. ARNOLD
Purdue University

THE PURPOSE of this paper is to discuss the components of a reading program for Mexican-American children. Although there are many factors in a good reading program, a few parts, important in any reading program for any child, are vital for Mexican-American children if they are going to learn to read satisfactorily.

The following nine questions are offered for the reader's consideration. If one is working in a reading program for Mexican-American children, the answers to these questions should be "yes." If not, the questions should be examined.

*Has a good learning environment been established?* This question is directed primarily to teachers, for it is the teacher who provides an atmosphere conducive to learning. Needed is a teacher who can accept children regardless of their background, culture, language, or social class. In short, children need a sensitive teacher who is willing to accept them as they are.

Teachers, by the very nature of their jobs, are placed in a position that has traditionally defined the teacher's role as the one who "makes children grow." The idea of making them grow implies standards of achievement. To be an accepting and achievement-oriented teacher does not necessarily suggest that the roles are incompatible. The important point is for the teacher to distinguish between a behavior and a person. The teacher can tell a child that a particular reading behavior was not attained and at the same time convey to the child that the behavior is in no way related to his individual worth. Children expect and can tolerate failure so long as they do not perceive the task as an integral part of their personality. To fail at a task is tolerable; to fail as a person is not.

Teachers often find themselves working with children from

101

backgrounds different from their own; hence, it becomes necessary for teachers to learn about the cultural and social class differences that may exist between the teacher and the child. Teachers of Mexican-American children must know the background of their students. Such awareness of their background can be learned from textbooks but it becomes truly meaningful when learned in the real world. Interacting with parents in the community and learning their values, their life styles, their pleasures, and their problems will provide insight into the lives of Mexican-American families. From such knowledge will come empathy for the children and a far deeper knowledge of their personal needs in the classroom. Such knowledge and understanding should result in improved classroom climate, a climate where individuals are accepted as worthwhile human beings who can and do learn. To be sure, at times certain reading behaviors are still not acquired and will need to be taught and received so that the child can achieve in both school and society.

*Is appropriate and worthwhile content used?* Regardless of methodology it is important that children read about something within their experiential repertoire; that is, they must bring a background of experience to the content of the printed page which, when read, will be something they can relate to and understand. In other words, children must not personally have experienced everything they read about; but unless they have a cognitive referent of some type, the author's message becomes irrelevant. Children understand best what they have seen, felt, or heard.

It is not at all clear what reading content will benefit Mexican-American children most. It seems important that they read about their culture and heritage, but it seems equally important that they be exposed to the body of knowledge expected to be learned by all children in our pluralistic, technological society. Reading in the content areas plays an extremely important role in the development of children especially after they have learned the fundamental skills of reading.

In the primary grades the content should be within the experiential background of the youngsters. However, reading content should be considered basically in terms of teaching reading skills. It is in the early school years that the children learn to break the code, analyze new words, and develop basic comprehension skills. The content of the story is worthwhile if it can be used as a vehicle to provide children opportunity to practice solving reading problems similar to those taught during the instructional period. Hopefully, authors can make the materials appropriate, relevant, and worthwhile; but first and foremost, the materials must be designed to reinforce instruction. Relevant reading can be done outside of the reading period, but practice reading must be done under supervision during the reading period.

*Are the readiness activities related to the reading materials?* Readiness is here defined in a broad sense to include the idea that every lesson has a short period of time preceding it in which the teacher and children can talk, questions can be asked, and judgments can be made concerning whether each child is ready to enter the new lesson. The teacher needs to know if the children can relate, respond, and react to the content of the story. A discussion using similar content gives the teacher the opportunity to determine if the children can handle the concepts covered in the story. The discussion will also provide an opportunity for the assessment of language development relevant to the concepts being presented. Thus, if the teacher decides that the children have the experiential, conceptual, and language background prerequisite for learning the lesson, he can then proceed with instruction. If the students have not attained the prerequisites, a readiness lesson will be more appropriate and probably more beneficial for a good learning experience.

*Is adequate expressive language participation provided?* Since Mexican-American children often lack English language proficiency, particularly upon entrance to school, practice in second-language learning appears to be an essential component of the reading and the broader language arts program. The language participation program can be viewed as a special case of readiness work, but it is so important to success in school achievement that it deserves special consideration.

Most Mexican-American children learn to understand English relatively easily. Yet frequently their ability in expressive English is quite low in comparison to their receptive English. This imbalance argues strongly for the need to develop skills in the use of English. The development of expressive English cannot be left to chance. To believe that children will be provided opportunity to use English through informal discussion without a structured language period appears to be unwise. The language program should be carefully designed to provide an expressive language base which will prepare the children to deal with school content in their second language. The relevance to reading is obvious.

Regardless of the actual content of a special language program, two very important dimensions of language are viewed as essential in the practice period. The study and practice of sounds in the language have long been recognized as essential if better spoken English is to be achieved. Certainly, if the objective of the teaching program is a socially unmarked dialect, one would place "sounds-oriented" exercises high on the priority list. The relationship of such an oral language program to phonics or decoding is easy to recognize.

The second part of an expressive language program, and equally as important as the phonological dimension, is the study and practice of language structures. The emphasis of this dimension should be on meaning, or understanding what is to be and what has been communicated. Children should learn how to manipulate words in utterances and how to take a basic idea and transform, elaborate, and express the thought in similar ways. The major objective would be to get children to talk in larger units: to get them to move away from monosyllabic, one word responses. The relationship of reading comprehension to language structures is apparent.

Other dimensions of language can be taught in a practice period just described. A good program should contain a balance between the development of phonology and the larger language elements in English. Without emphasis on both dimensions, the program will most likely be inadequate for many Mexican-American children learning English as their second language.

*Is the program sequentially organized to provide for continuous growth?* Most educators believe that reading should be taught in an organized manner and the material should be developmentally oriented, proceeding from simple to complex. If Mexican-American children have difficulty with reading because of a more fundamental language-based problem, then focus must be placed on the language the children are learning as well as the usual reading sequence. A teacher of middle class children from homes where English is the language spoken does not have to place such strong emphasis on language development because the children come to school with reasonably good command of the language of instruction.

With non-native English speakers it becomes extremely important that the teacher determine the extent to which the children can work with the new vocabulary presented. But perhaps equally or even more important is whether the child can work with new or modified language structures. As of now it is not known what structures should be taught and what sequence should be followed. Research in the area of second language learning is vitally needed to establish a developmental sequence of English vocabulary and syntax as well as to determine naturalistic language structures the children can work with easily. Then the oral language sequence can be carefully correlated with the sequence of skills being taught in reading.

*Is provision made for individual differences within the reading program?* Educators today almost universally acknowledge the concept of individual differences, but frequently the concept is not fully realized. Perhaps it is due to the fact that people do not know how to assess individual differences. Evaluation and diagnostic teaching are of paramount importance if each child is to be given an opportunity to learn at his developmental rate. Behavioral psychologists have contributed much that can be applied to reading. They have pointed out the need to establish behavioral objectives which are easily assessed by the teacher. If observable reading behaviors are set as objectives, evaluation is much easier. Diagnosis based on observable behaviors can naturally lead to prescriptive teaching of individuals.

Assessment of individual attainment based on observation of specific behaviors can, of course, be accomplished through testing and other formal evaluation methods. However, informal evaluation by teachers is also needed, such as the informal assessment of specific behaviors in the readiness period preceding the lesson. It is then the teachers can make judgments as to whether the children have attained the prerequisite behaviors needed for the next lesson. If the behaviors were not attained, then provision for additional re-teaching must be made.

*Is extensive training in areas of weaknesses available?* When a teacher discovers a child has a weakness, a plan of corrective action needs to be implemented. To acknowledge that a child has a weakness and not to teach to remove the weakness can be a self-defeating situation that makes both the child and his teacher frustrated and unhappy. Thus, schools have the enormous task of providing adequate corrective work for each child.

The types of remedial activities will be numerous, for children can have many different problems. Problems may be directly related to reading or they may be reading-related, all of which must be dealt with if successful reading achievement is the goal for all children. There will be not only special reading instruction but also language, perceptual, motor, and cognitive skills programs.

A good remedial program calls for a highly individualized plan of corrective work in the classroom in conjunction with special remedial programs provided by the school through ancillary, special service personnel such as paraprofessionals, remedial teachers, and school psychologists. The task of providing extensive remedial work is expensive and very demanding; but if Mexican-American children have the right to read, then the problem must be faced squarely and ways found to provide for corrective work.

*Does the reading program provide for systematic evaluation of the child as well as the program itself?* The importance of informal assessment by the classroom teacher has been mentioned. Unfortunately, with the particular problems that Mexican-American children have, the standardized tests available are nearly useless. Even basic content validity of many achievement tests is subject to serious question. The implication is quite clear: objective measures of growth and achievement are greatly needed for Mexican-American children. Teachers need to know if the children have learned what has been presented in the lessons. If an experimental method is used, the need is even more pressing. Not only pupil progress but also program effectiveness needs to be evaluated. The value of an experimental reading program is highly questionable unless some sort of objective measures can be used to evaluate effectiveness. Thus, it is necessary for program developers not only to build new curriculum materials but also to find ways to assess pupil attainment.

The concept of mastery tests has much to offer those in reading. Children are not measured against one another but are tested to see if they have learned the skills. In experimental situations groups of children are assessed to determine if they have learned the reading behaviors identified as critical for continued success in reading.

*Are children assured successful reading experiences?* The final point is concerned with happy experiences. When a person has a happy or a successful experience in any endeavor he undertakes, he will enjoy and be predisposed to return to that endeavor. That generalization holds true for reading, too. Sometimes teachers try so hard to get children to learn that the learning task becomes frustrating and unpleasant. Children tune the teacher out and are turned off. No matter how good the reading program is and how conscientious, dedicated, and hardworking the teacher may be, if "tune out-turn off" occurs, the children and the reading program are likely to fail.

A good reading period has enough flexibility to include opportunities for children to work on tasks that they are ready to learn. Insuring successful reading experiences, insofar as is humanly possible, will predispose the children to want to read and ultimately will lead to proficient and enjoyable reading. This then is a plea to make reading a happy experience for boys and girls, especially for Mexican-American children who in many cases have had more than their share of unhappy experiences.

Nine components which have been identified appear to be fundamental for an effective reading program. If educators can answer "yes" to the nine questions posed, it seems that their reading program has a good chance of being an effective and successful one, one that has the major components needed for a reading program for Mexican-American children.

# Characteristics of Gifted and Creative Pupils and Their Needs for Reading Experience*

PAUL A. WITTY, Emeritus
Northwestern University

WITH THE ADVENT of the intelligence test and its widespread use, attention in American schools was directed to the wide range of abilities within every classroom and the consequent need for adaptations and extensions of the curriculum. Efforts to care for individual differences were attempted to varying degrees in almost all schools. Special provisions were initiated for slow learning and retarded pupils, and occasional efforts were designed to enrich the experience of the gifted (1).

Generally accepted was the concept of the gifted child as an individual of high IQ, a conviction that has long persisted in education. The comprehensive studies of Terman, following the pioneer work of Binet, resulted in the testing of large numbers of children and youth and the assigning of IQs to various categories of ability. Children earning IQs of 130 and higher were designated as "gifted." Such children constituted about 1 percent of elementary school pupils in the early surveys, while somewhat higher percentages were later reported.

About 1920, large scale genetic investigations of the gifted were undertaken. In 1921, Terman and his associates started a search for 1,000 gifted pupils. They were able to locate about 1,500 such subjects. Then they sought to study them and to answer two questions:

1. What traits characterize these pupils?
2. What kinds of adults do they become?

Reports of these studies were published in several volumes and were

* Reprinted from Paul A. Witty, Editor, *Reading for the Gifted and the Creative Student.* International Reading Association, Newark, Delaware, 1971, 5-18.

summarized by Terman and Oden (15). In a magazine article, Terman stated that the following findings were the most significant. Children of IQ 140 and above are superior to unselected children in physical development, social adjustment, character traits, and educational attainment. The typical pupil in the group had "mastered the school subjects to a point about two grades beyond the one in which he was enrolled, some of them three or four grades beyond" (14). Moreover, Terman stated that not one of his findings had been disproved in many years of research. Indeed, the basic conclusions of Terman concerning the superiority of gifted children in physical and social adjustment, as well as in educational attainment, were corroborated by studies made by the present writer and others (20).

Genetic studies included follow-up investigations over a period of 30 years. These studies showed that the academic superiority of gifted pupils was maintained and that "the promise of youth" was realized to a conspicuous degree. Terman and Oden found that nearly 90 percent entered college and 70 percent were graduated. About one-third were given honors and approximately two-thirds continued in graduate study (15).

Further investigation of the gifted as young adults, as well as study of proven geniuses, convinced Terman that ". . . the genius who achieves the highest eminence is one whom intelligence tests would have identified as gifted in childhood" (14).

Although the results of the writer's studies of children of high IQ resembled closely the findings of Terman, he differed sharply in the interpretation of the data. He questioned whether one is justified in assuming that a high IQ may be used to predict creative behavior or the achievements of "genius." Moreover, he stressed the importance of factors such as interest, drive, opportunity, and early education in affecting the nature and extent of individual attainment.

## Characteristics of Gifted Children

These genetic studies have presented a clear-cut picture of the gifted child (20). Confirmation of the findings has led to the general acceptance of the following description of the verbally gifted child: The gifted child was found to be better developed physically than

the average child of his age. He was also somewhat superior to unselected pupils in his social adjustment. He was clearly not a peculiar, social misfit.

The educational attainment of the gifted child in the elementary
school was *generally* accelerated. His best achievement was in reading and language; his poorest, in writing and spelling. In Witty's
studies (*21*) 50 percent of the pupils in his group learned to read
before they started school; almost 40 percent, before they were five;
and some, as early as three or four years of age. Their vocabulary
was remarkably accelerated; thus a ten-year old pupil said, "Flaunt
means to show or display with intent to show." And Mars was defined
as "a planet, god of war, also a verb."

Rapidity in learning also characterized the gifted who acquired
academic skills in about half the time allotted to them. In the upper
grades of the elementary school, the gifted child had mastered the
curriculum to a degree two or more full grades beyond the average
for his class. Although the gifted were found in all social and racial
groups, they were most frequently located in homes of high social
and economic levels.

Certainly, these studies of gifted pupils demonstrated the value
of the IQ in selecting one type of child for whom promise is great and
for whom appropriate opportunities are needed. Moreover, it became abundantly clear that enrichment, such as that offered in
special classes which have been provided in the elementary and in
the secondary school, has proved beneficial. Yet the amount of such
offerings has been, and continues to be, meager. For example, in
the field of reading, disadvantaged and disabled pupils have been
increasingly given special help, but rarely is such consideration ac-
corded the gifted pupil. This tendency may readily be seen by
examining the approaches and materials used in high school and
college classes for reading improvement, as well as in the amount and
nature of special provisions in elementary school classes.

## Failure to Recognize the Importance of Early Learning

Terman and his associates emphasized the importance of hereditary factors in producing relatively stable IQs. Although educators

mentioned the significance of opportunities for early learning, their studies dealt largely with pupils of school age after the crucial years of early childhood had passed. Recently, the importance of the early years has been brought dramatically to our attention. Thus Pines (*12*) has stated:

> Millions of children are being irreparably damaged by our failure to stimulate them intellectually during their crucial years—from birth to six. Millions of others are being held back from their true potential.

Without doubt, there has been neglect of intellectual stimulation for young children in the home and in the nursery school or preschool center. It is being recognized that the provision of rich and varied experience in early childhood will increase learning ability and may heighten intelligence ratings. Some writers believe that the provision of such conditions would raise the number of superior children to be found in areas in which deprivation and disadvantage prevail. Improvement might also transpire in other groups provided similar opportunities. Thus, Hunt (*11*) has indicated that "it might become feasible to raise the average level of intelligence—by a substantial degree . . . this 'substantial degree' might be of the order of 30 points of IQ."

It has been shown that extreme environmental changes do affect IQs. No longer is the IQ looked upon as a result chiefly of hereditary factors and, hence, considered unchangeable. The pendulum has swung to an emphasis on environment, and the importance of early learning has been stressed. Accordingly, programs to improve intelligence have been proposed by several writers (*2, 5*).

Although research should be undertaken to test claims and hypotheses, it has already been shown that programs of early learning have led to remarkable attainments in reading and language proficiency.

## Children Who Read Early

Investigators have recently stressed the potentiality of most children for learning to read at early ages. The possibility was long ago recognized by scholars who suggested that perhaps the time which was most desirable for beginning reading instruction was age four. But opposition was great to this suggestion since most educators appeared to believe that "readiness" for reading necessitated the attainment of a mental age of six years or more. In 1966, the appearance of Durkin's study (4) of children who read early caused many thoughtful people to reexamine this issue. The children in a group who read early entered the first grade with superior achievement and maintained their lead over a five-year period. Notable was Durkin's description of the parents of the early readers. They were characterized by a respect for learning and its encouragement in very young children.

The parents of gifted children who read early, in the writer's studies made in the Psycho-Educational Clinic of Northwestern University, appeared to be similarly concerned about the achievement of their children during the early crucial years. These parents frequently read aloud to their children, fostered language expression, provided varied books and materials, and showed by their own behavior a profound respect for reading. Some parents encouraged their children to write, spell, or record their experiences in simple forms. Under these conditions, more than half of the gifted group learned, without undue pressure, to read before starting to school.

Several studies have revealed the possibility of children's making remarkable progress in reading and language development during the preschool period. Thus, Terman (15) reported that one of the gifted girls in his study demonstrated on tests that she could read almost as well "at the age of twenty-five months as the average child at the end of the first grade." And one gifted boy, observed by the writer, started to read at home when he was four. He had read almost all books in the *Golden First Adventures in Learning* series (Western Publishing Company) before he entered kindergarten. His favorite, the *Thinking Book*, had fostered creative expression. This boy's parents not only encouraged him to read but also offered him appropriate materials. It is possible that the provision of abundant resources and conditions similar to those found in the homes of children who read early would result in increasing the number of gifted children at the time of school entrance, since reading and language proficiencies are important factors in intelligent behavior. Certainly, this is a possibility and a hope of utmost importance for the welfare of society.

## Reading for Verbally Gifted Pupils

One of the greatest needs of the verbally gifted child involves the provision of individually appropriate reading experiences from the beginning of his school entrance. If he is able to read on entering the first grade, he should be encouraged to do so from varied reading sources that are individually suitable and appealing. In every class, provision should be made and guidance offered so that the gifted pupil who knows how to read will continue to develop his reading abilities and to apply them widely.

Since some verbally gifted pupils will be able to read on entering the kindergarten, opportunities should also be provided to enable them to develop and apply their reading skills at this time.

We should recognize that reading for enjoyment is a legitimate feature of a developmental reading program for gifted children. To achieve this goal, a variety of printed materials should be made available to enable these children to find genuine satisfaction in the extension and enrichment of their interests.

The following procedure has been found helpful in guiding the reading of the gifted pupil. It requires the administration of an interest inventory to the members of an entire class. Small groups of children with common interests are identified, and reading materials of varying difficulty are made available in accord with the differences in ability within each interest group. Thus, each child may select and share his discoveries from reading material of a suitable level. In this situation, the gifted child makes his contribution from reading challenging sources of appropriate difficulty.

Extensive use of children's literature may provide further extension of interests. Gifted children, as studies have shown, usually have varied and rich interests. They collect• stamps, coins, and specimens of many kinds; they frequently explore animal, bird, and plant life; they enjoy following discoveries in outer space; and in other ways reveal a large number of interests. They sometimes cultivate an interest which affords the basis of a lifelong pursuit or vocation. Their interests often grow into hobbies followed for several years. There are, of course, some gifted children whose backgrounds are impoverished and who need to be encouraged to develop and cultivate worthy interest patterns. For these children, as for others, the use of an interest inventory may yield clues of significance. These interests offer a rich resource for motivating gifted children to read widely and with deep satisfaction. When one observes the happiness children experience in reading materials associated with their strong interests, one appreciates more fully the truth of the poet John Masefield's remark, "The days that make us happy make us wise."

These procedures will prove helpful in fostering the development of effective reading in the verbally gifted. With differences in emphasis, the suggestions will prove effective also with creative pupils.

### Identification of the Creative Pupil

It has become clear that the use of standard tests of intelligence will not enable one to identify the creative pupil with a high degree of success. Recognition of this fact is not new. Indeed, many years ago, the writer found that the correlation between IQ and performance judged to be highly creative was low. He suggested that the materials generally utilized in the intelligence test are not suitable to elicit original, imaginative, or creative responses. Undoubtedly, the intelligence test has helped in the identification of one kind of ability, but it will not enable one to locate creative pupils with accuracy. Several investigators have found that if one were to delimit his selection to pupils of IQ 130 plus, he would fail to include many of the most creative pupils. Accordingly, efforts have been made to develop tests of creativity. An examination of the procedures employed by investigators such as Getzels and Jackson (7) will readily reveal the complexity of giving and scoring these instruments. Although study and development of measures of creativity are highly desirable in experimental situations, the tests usually are impractical for classroom use.

Critics have stressed certain limitations in the tests of creativity and the need for caution in using them. Such criticism undoubtedly will lead to extension of the studies and clarification of important issues. Particularly needed is further study of various kinds of creativity, their measurement, and their relationships. As Guilford (9) states:

> It would be risky to conclude that because a child shows signs of creativity in art he should also be creative in mathematics or in science, or vice versa.

## Techniques for Identifying Creative Pupils

Despite the limitations of tests of creativity, there are a number of practical approaches which are being employed advantageously to identify and encourage children whose promise of creativity is great. For example, in a study made by the writer, the remarkable film photographed by Arne Sucksdorff, *The Hunter and the Forest,* was shown in many schools throughout the United States. The film has no commentary but utilizes a musical score and the sounds of animals and birds as accompaniments.

After the pupils had seen the film, they were asked to write a commentary, a story, or a poem about it. Approximately 10 percent of the pupils wrote so effectively that their products suggested unique creative ability, as judged by three "experts." If a high IQ had been used to identify the gifted, a majority of these pupils would have been excluded. Moreover, many of the outstanding compositions were written by pupils who had not previously been observed as having unusual aptitude in writing. If additional outstanding performance corroborated this first demonstration of exceptional ability, these pupils would be considered potentially gifted in this area.

Because of such findings, the writer proposed that a potentially gifted child be considered as any child whose performance in a worthwhile type of human endeavor is repeatedly or consistently remarkable. He suggested that a search be made not only for pupils of high verbal ability but also for those of promise in mathematics and science, writing, art, music, drama, mechanical ability, and social leadership.

Scholars are increasingly recognizing the prevalence of undiscovered talent and are stressing the presence of multiple talents in children and youth. For example, Taylor (13) has described a multiple talent search by the *Utah Task Force*. He points out that there are many types of talent and indicates that if one's search is limited to a single talent area, such as communication talents, one might include about 50 percent of the pupils who would be above average. When six talent areas are employed, about 90 percent of the pupils would be above average in at least one area. This promising approach for selecting talented pupils needs to be studied further to determine its validity and practicality.

## Differences Between the Gifted and the Creative

The writer has already noted some of the characteristics of gifted children who have been identified by intelligence tests. In addition to their superiority in school work and related activities, they were found to be well-adjusted socially and to get along well with their peers. Creative pupils differed markedly from the verbally gifted in these respects. It should be observed, however, that verbally gifted pupils also exhibit almost every type of social maladjustment; but the incidence is not frequent when compared with the number in the general population. Moreover, it is much lower than in groups of creative pupils. Torrance (18) has stressed the problems in adjustment faced by creative pupils. He points out that when an individual has a *new* idea, he becomes immediately a minority of one. The independence of mind of the creative pupil implies a nonconformity to group pressures, a condition which often leads to adjustment problems. Torrance states that "In no group thus far studied have we failed to find relatively clear evidence of the operation of pressures against the most creative members of the group . . ." (18).

Thus, many highly creative pupils may become "disturbing elements" in the classroom.

The findings of Torrance are supported by a remarkable study of talented persons made by Victor and Mildred G. Goertzel (8). These authors chose 400 persons acknowledged as "eminent" by a high frequency of biographies currently written about them. After studying the childhood of the subjects, the Goertzels reported that almost all were early readers. Moreover, they were original in their thinking but impatient with routine. They were often rejected by their peers. Three out of five experienced serious problems in school. The Goertzels conclude:

> Now as in the days of the Four Hundred, the child who is both
> intelligent and creative remains society's most valuable resource.
> When we learn to work with him instead of against him, his
> talents may reward us in ways beyond our ability to imagine.

It may readily be seen that the teacher has an unusual opportunity to help the creative pupil meet personal and social problems through reading. Not only will wide reading enable him to gain information to satisfy and extend his interests but it may also aid him to meet personal and social problems with greater success as well as to build an appropriate ideal of self (19). Following are suggestions for satisfying some of the needs of the gifted and the creative pupil through reading.

## Reading for the Gifted and the Creative

Earlier the writer stressed some needs of one type of the gifted, namely, pupils of high verbal ability. The following suggestions apply not only to such pupils but also to others who display various kinds of creativity. Both types are referred to as "gifted" in the following discussion.

Provisions are needed for a widespread installation of programs for early education. Such programs should prove beneficial for most children since the early years constitute the period when learning is most rapid. Abilities of many kinds may be nourished through offering varied early opportunities for acquiring information and skills. It has been suggested that the early years may prove to be the optimal time to initiate instruction in reading and related language acquisitions. Creativity may also be cultivated profitably during these crucial years. There is a pressing need for establishing centers for early learning throughout our country in which reading will have high priority.

It has been shown that many gifted children can read on entering the kindergarten and the first grade. At this time, they should be given opportunities to develop and use widely their reading skills. During the primary grades, routine basal reading instruction should be replaced by a balanced program adapted to differences in abilities and interests.

The interests of gifted pupils should be employed to motivate reading. The teacher who advocates individualized reading may help pupils to satisfy their interests by making accessible a wide assortment of reading materials. Teachers who follow the language-experience approach often make an important contribution, too, by leading children to prepare, read, and share their own "books." In the classes of skilled teachers, the interests and abilities of gifted pupils develop rapidly. By the time they reach the fourth grade, they will typically have become avid readers. Effective teachers provide additional motivation through associating reading with carefully selected films, filmstrips, and TV programs. Teachers and librarians can work effectively together in behalf of the gifted. Sometimes, they use interest inventories as a basis for the suggestion of more appropriate and diversified reading.

Several writers have stressed the gifted child's need for added experience in critical reading throughout the intermediate grades and the high school. And others have emphasized his need for reading experience to help him meet his personal and social problems. The reading of narratives and biographies may help gifted pupils to deal more successfully with problems as they arise. Although pupils may not be helped by reading alone, such reading may prove beneficial, particularly if it is associated with discussion and related experiences. In many cases it has been remarkably effective. For example, *Amos Fortune: Free Man* by Elizabeth Yates provided the basis for a wholesome identification of a discouraged boy with the central character in the story who met successfully problems similar to his own difficulties. The influence of several biographies about Thomas Jefferson inspired a gifted child to remark, "Everyone should read about the many things this man did to make his country great. Each of us ought to be able to do something, especially when we realize what one man was able to do."

A gifted boy, on his way to becoming a competent historian, read many of the books in the *Landmark* and the *World Landmark* series and critically analyzed their authenticity by comparing them with other biographies. He was greatly influenced by Genevieve Foster's association of the times with each historical character's life. After he had read widely, the boy stated that he was convinced that biography is "our only real history."

Gifted children should be encouraged to enjoy poetry, an area of reading sometimes neglected by them. They should be given opportunities to write poetry, too. Their products are often superior; in addition, their writing sometimes reveals pressing individual problems or needs. From the first, children should have access to collections of poetry. Very young children in our studies were found to enjoy the writing of Dr. Seuss and A. A. Milne. In the junior and senior high schools, students liked the verse of Ogden Nash, Arthur Guiterman, and many other poets, such as Millay, Frost, Dickinson, and Sandburg.

Gifted children should have opportunities to enjoy humorous presentations. Some books depict hilarious situations which gifted pupils have found engaging. The humor of Robert McCloskey's *Homer Price* was almost universally appreciated by these elementary school pupils. Gifted pupils will seek out and enjoy other humorous books if they are given an opportunity to read extensively. There will be a wide range of choices, but favorites will probably include the Seuss books, Disney illustrated publications, *Mr. Popper's Penguins* by Richard and Florence Atwater, the appealing nonsense in Walter R. Brooks' *Freddy Books,* and the comical adventures of Hugh Lofting's *Dr. Doolittle.*

The guidance of reading continues to be a responsibility of the teacher in the high school. In order to offer assistance to gifted pupils who are in need of improved reading skills, the teacher should first ascertain the pupil's reading status. Testing should proceed periodically throughout the elementary and secondary school. Specific plans for building skills should then be worked out for each pupil in accord with his interests and needs. Gifted pupils often need experience in reading critically throughout their school careers. They need to examine and evaluate the meanings and possible interpretations of printed materials of various kinds. They should be encouraged also to read widely and to enjoy reading.

It is unfortunate that reading improvement courses for the high school student seldom stress critical reading and creative response. Too much attention is usually allotted to speed reading or to repeating facts rather than to examining the authenticity, implications, and significance of printed materials.

Scholars stress the fact that a great stimulation would be given to the education of the gifted, as well as to education generally, by a widespread inauguration of programs in creative reading. Creative reading may be regarded as the highest and most neglected type of reading. We may think of one type of reading as simple comprehension involving accurate identification of words and other thought units. For this type of reading, emphasis on skills such as getting the central thought of a passage or noting details is appropriate. These responses are to a marked degree *convergent* in nature. Only to a small degree do they extend beyond the facts presented and become *divergent* in nature. In creative reading, *divergent* response is stressed. Relationships among facts are examined, and interpretations are drawn. As Torrance (*17*) states,

> When a person reads creatively, he is sensitive to problems and possibilities in whatever he reads. He makes himself aware of the gaps in knowledge, the unsolved problems, the missing elements, things that are incomplete or out of focus. To resolve this tension, so important in the creative thinking process, the creative reader sees new relationships, creates new combinations, synthesizes relatively unrelated elements into a coherent whole, redefines or transforms certain pieces of information to discover new uses, and builds onto what is known.

## The Role of the Teacher

The teacher who guides the reading of gifted children will need to become informed about the development of children and youth and should be skilled in using child study techniques, such as the interest inventory. The teacher should also become thoroughly acquainted with literature for children and youth and should work closely with parents and librarians in obtaining suitable and varied materials to satisfy the interests and meet the needs of gifted and creative pupils. The teacher may be helped by the study of anthologies of literature for children and youth and by the examination of booklists. These teachers should read widely and communicate to pupils their enthusiasm and pleasure in reading.

Teachers of the gifted and creative student should be broadly informed about poetry. Some teachers are introducing gifted pupils to poetry from collections. To stimulate an interest in poetry, many others are using recordings, and some are becoming skilled in reading aloud favorite selections to foster enjoyment of poetry. Further enjoyment of poetry may be engendered by encouraging children to write poetry. Proficiency in telling stories is also a characteristic of the stimulating teacher.

In recent years, there has been a prolonged search for *the* most efficient method to teach beginning reading. Repeatedly, it has been found that successful instruction accompanies the use of varied methods and that no single method is conspicuously superior to other methods.

Occasionally, a glimpse of the recognition of the importance of factors other than "methods" is found in a comparative study. The writer believes that failure to consider the characteristics and practices of the teacher is a great weakness in the study of "methods." His belief is substantiated by Chall's most perceptive report (3) of her impression based on her observations of more than ten different classes and teachers using various methods of reading instruction:

> How interested pupils are in learning to read, I concluded, is not determined by what method or set of materials they are using. I saw excitement, enthusiasm, and general interest ex-

hibited in classes using every reading program. I also saw children respond to each with listlessness, apathy, boredom, restlessness.

Generally, it is what the teacher did with the method, the materials, and the children rather than the method itself that seemed to make the difference.

## Summary

Few schools have comprehensive reading programs for gifted and creative students. There is a neglect of such pupils as attention and opportunities are increasingly offered to the "disadvantaged" and other exceptional groups. There are, of course, many gifted pupils among the disadvantaged who should be identified and helped to realize their potentialities. Reading offers for all gifted and creative pupils an avenue by which potentialities may be more fully realized and satisfactions may be heightened.

In this chapter, the writer has defined and described gifted and creative students and has indicated some of their most insistent needs for reading instruction and related experiences. The need for more adequate teacher-training is stressed. In the following chapter, brief descriptions will be given of reading and language programs which are being developed and employed to satisfy these needs. It will be noted that diversity is the chief characteristic of these programs and that theory and practice vary widely from school to school. It is notable also that the work of Guilford (10) on the structure of intellect has deeply influenced the development of several programs which emphasize divergent thinking as well as evaluation. The variety and richness of the practices should enable the teacher to find suggestions which can be employed rewardingly in fostering thinking skills so frequently neglected in the past in reading and language instruction.

## REFERENCES

1.  Barbe, Walter B. *Psychology and Education of the Gifted: Selected Readings.* New York: Appleton-Century-Crofts, 1965.

2. Beck, Joan. *How to Raise a Brighter Child*. New York: Trident Press, 1967.
3. Chall, Jeanne S. *Learning to Read: The Great Debate*. New York:McGraw-Hill, 1967.
4. Durkin, Dolores. *Children Who Read Early*. New York: Teachers College Press, Columbia University, 1966.
5. Engelmann, Siegfried, and Therese Engelmann. *Give Your Child a Superior Mind*. New York: Simon and Schuster, 1966.
6. Gallagher, James J. *Teaching the Gifted Child*. Boston: Allyn and Bacon, 1964.
7. Getzels, J. W., and P. W. Jackson. *Creativity and Intelligence*. New York: John Wiley and Sons, 1962.
8. Goertzel, Victor, and Mildred G. Goertzel. *Cradles of Eminence*. Boston: Little, Brown, 1962.
9. Guilford, J. P. "Potentiality for Creativity," *Gifted Child Quarterly*, 6 (Autumn 1962).
10. Guilford, J. P. "Structure of Intellect," *Psychological Bulletin*, 53, 1956.
11. Hunt, J. McV. *Intelligence and Experience*. New York: Ronald Press, 1961.
12. Pines, Maya. *Revolution in Learning—The Years from Birth to Six*. New York: Harper and Row, 1967.
13. Taylor, Calvin W. "Multiple Talent Search," *The Instructor*, April 1968.
14. Terman, Lewis M. "The Discovery and Encouragement of Exceptional Talent," *American Psychologist*, 9 (June 1954).
15. Terman, Lewis M., and Melita H. Oden. *The Gifted Child Grows Up*. Stanford, California: Stanford University Press, 1947.
16. Torrance, E. Paul. "Explorations in Creative Thinking," *Education*, 81 (December 1960).
17. Torrance, E. Paul. *Gifted Children in the Classroom*. New York: Macmillan, 1965.
18. Torrance, E. Paul. "Problems of Highly Creative Children," *Gifted Child Quarterly*, 5 (Summer 1961).
19. Witty, Paul A. "Reading for the Gifted," in J. Allen Figurel (Ed.), *Reading and Realism*, 1968 Proceedings, Volume 13, Part 1. Newark, Delaware: International Reading Association, 1969.
20. Witty, Paul A. (Ed.). *The Gifted Child*. Boston: D. C. Heath, 1951.
21. Witty, Paul A. "Who Are the Gifted?" *Education for the Gifted*, Fifty-seventh Yearbook of the National Society for the Study of Education, Part II. Chicago: University of Chicago Press, 1958.

# Improving Flexibility in Reading for the Advanced Student

ONETA R. FURR
Midwestern University

PLANNING for elementary reading instruction should begin with the student. Identification of student needs requires careful diagnosis to determine levels of achievement, types of interests, and sources of motivation within the group. The planning of a meaningful program of reading instruction can then be accomplished in terms of the information revealed by the diagnosis.

## Identification of the Advanced Student

The advanced student is in special need of early identification. Such a student is usually reading above grade level and has an elevated score on intelligence tests. The advanced student will likely have learned by many different methods. An example was Stephen, five and one-half years, who said, "I didn't have to learn to read—I just always knew how." On investigation the mother revealed that she first noticed Stephen reading the titles of the records as he played them on his record player at three and one-half years. Stephen had associated the words in the titles with the words he heard on the records. He soon was reading stories that had been read to him several times. Thus, his keen interest in words and his retention, both visual and auditory, provided clues to his intellectual potential and his advancement as a reader.

Classroom observation, which may confirm test results, is another useful means by which the advanced student can be recognized. Students who demonstrate unusual powers of concentration, have superior command of language, enjoy a keen sense of humor, learn quickly, recall accurately, exercise exceptional powers of observation, see relationships, and can effectively approach the solution of practical problems are likely to be mentally above average. In addition, a survey of favorite television programs, books, magazines, and leisure time activities will often identify students with broad, mature interests and a marked desire to learn (4). Although there are some overachievers in reading, they are comparatively few. The large majority of advanced readers tend to come from the advanced student group. It is for this reason that the present discussion will give major consideration to the advanced student as the primary source from which advanced readers are developed.

Quality diagnosis is the beginning of quality instruction. As Whipple points out, "No good plan for reading can be carried out until the teacher knows his pupils well" (2). Becoming acquainted with pupils requires time, effort, interest, and proper evaluation. Teacher diagnosis of student needs involves the accumulation of information which leads to the development of insights regarding the reader's functioning skill level, the nature and quality of his stored information, and his psychological characteristics. Valuable information for instruction may be gleaned from a knowledge of the makeup of the child's own private world. The type and breadth of his interests and the economic, educational, and cultural levels of his home and community are highly important factors. The extent to which he is accepted as a worthy member of his family and his peer group, as well as the state of his physical health and well-being, must likewise be considered. Such elements are of great significance in the planning of reading instruction for all students, whether advanced or not.

## Working with the Advanced Reader

The advanced student in reading, at whatever level, poses a challenge even to a discerning teacher. There may be a tendency on the part of the teacher to neglect the individual who "can make it on his own." The development of a versatile or flexible reader, however, requires careful attention. Although the able student may forge ahead on his own initiative, his progress can be enhanced by the skillful direction of a capable, understanding teacher. For example, the advanced student may tend to memorize the beginning reading vocabulary. By the time he reaches the third or fourth grade the reading vocabulary load becomes too great for memorization, with the result that the individual is in danger of becoming disabled in spite of his beginning potential. A student's ability to proceed satisfactorily "on his own" becomes substantially limited under such circumstances. He begins to suffer the consequences of having to proceed without the benefits of skilled direction by a capable teacher.

Likewise, in developing study skills and critical reading skills the advanced reader may profit greatly from the benefits of skillful instruction. Although he may be reading satisfactorily at his own level, he is more likely to progress toward reading maturity when he is properly guided. Teachers must provide challenging and enriching reading experiences. A creative and imaginative teacher who has instructional expertise in reading is essential if the capable student is to fulfill his reading potential.

The need of the advanced reader is for guidance of a somewhat different nature than that given to his less gifted fellows. Fundamental skills should be developed sequentially but at a faster rate than is usually expected. Vocabulary development, word recognition skills, oral reading, comprehension, purposeful reading, and the reading study skills must all move forward in a spiral fashion with no limits set by grade level. The important consideration in teacher and/or student evaluation is whether there has been progress since the previous evaluation.

Caution should be exercised in planning reading activities for the advanced student. Assignments must be purposeful and appropriate to the achievement level and interest of the student. Opportunities to participate in group discussions, to profit from the insights of classmates, to check the validity of the reader's own thinking, and to learn to express ideas in a social situation are very important. The use of basal readers makes it possible for the advanced student to react at a high level of interpretation because of his awareness of implied meanings. Supplementary reading activities can extend ideas acquired in basal reading and can enrich class discussions.

Time should be provided for the advanced reader to read self-selected materials that satisfy his personal needs and curiosities. He can be guided in the selection of many types of materials and at different levels of difficulty. At no time should the advanced student be allowed to settle for minimum requirements.

The advanced student in reading needs exposure to materials of great number and variety. A pressing question facing teachers today is which materials can best be utilized to serve a particular student's need? The library has become a materials center or learning center where books and magazines are only a part of available resources. Audio tapes, filmstrips, and programed learning materials are especially useful in challenging the capable student.

Certain responsibilities for promoting optimum development of advanced readers rest with the school. The general school environment should allow reasonable freedom of functioning for students in a cooperatively developed reading program. The school schedule must accommodate teacher-student conferences, as well as formal and informal evaluation. Such evaluations can result in the refinement of skills, the setting of further goals, and the selection of procedures and materials to be utilized.

## Flexibility in Reading

Analysis of the characteristics of advanced readers indicates they have a repertory of reading skills and an ability to use appropriate skills for their purpose and the material (4). Such readers are skillful in adjusting method and rate to their purposes for reading, thus showing unusual flexibility. Flexibility in reading is a key to the reading maturity and efficiency which characterize the able reader. According to McDonald there are at least three identifiable characteristics of the flexible reader: 1) He reads with a definite purpose; 2) he adapts his reading approaches to variations in style, content, difficulty of vocabulary, and his own background of knowledge; and 3) he is emotionally free to look beyond the printed lines to the meanings that are implied (1).

In order to improve flexibility, students should be made aware of certain rate adjustment approaches. The characteristics and application of each approach should be part of the fundamentals of a basic reading program. Four identifiable techniques include skimming (reading swiftly and lightly); scanning (reading rapidly for main ideas); study reading (reading with maximum understanding); and reflective reading (following directions, enjoying poetry). Planned instruction and assessment, together with opportunities for declaring purposes and practice in applying different techniques to different materials, should provide an understanding of each approach. The steadily enlarging store of knowledge in all fields necessitates a careful appraisal of possible ways to improve reading efficiency.

Recent research challenges the widely prevalent concept that the reader can deliberately and consciously vary his reading approach and reading rate. In one study of 6,000 elementary-to-adult readers 90 percent maintained a characteristic approach to almost all types of reading, despite instructions for changes in purpose and variation in material (1). Further research on advanced readers may furnish clues as to how efficiency, flexibility, and maturity in reading are attained. Can each of these goals be taught as a separate act? At present, research suggests that flexibility is a very complex reading activity which involves a number of differing but related factors. This view is in contrast with the concept of flexibility as being one inclusive ability or skill. It may be possible that reading efficiency, flexibility, and maturity are by-products of the reading-thinking approach to instruction. That is, the key is possibly to be found within the cognitive process, rather than in the conscious use of flexibility as a learned skill.

## Reading as Thinking

Reading and thinking cannot be divorced from each other. Recognition of this fact may give new light in which to consider the nature of flexibility. Reading and thinking are mental processes. In terms of the written word, both are necessary to an understanding of the writer's message. Reading is a process based on the experience and knowledge of the reader and his desire to find out. Reading, like thinking, involves continual change (3). The reader interacts with the printed ideas, sequence, problems, and solutions. He reads to test his purposes and his assumptions. His ability to perform critically and creatively, his level of maturity, his declared purposes, and the nature and difficulty of the material are all important elements of the cognitive aspect of the reading-thinking process.

Flexibility results when an individual reader knows what he wants, knows how to get what he wants by reading, and is willing to persevere to accomplish his purpose. Hence, an urgent need of students today is to acquire compelling motives for worthwhile personal reading (3). It can be seen that the reader's purpose reflects his experience, his knowledge, and his motivation. Sound reading instruction must elicit maximum student participation and vigorous intellectual effort at all levels.

In light of the apparent present knowledge and experience, the teacher's task is that of giving emphasis to reading as thinking, while at the same time insuring a sound reading foundation. For the advanced student—and all others—the basic reading foundation will include the following: First, efficient tools such as word analysis, location skills, study skills, and organization skills; second, many and varied reading materials such as books, visuals, auditory items, and graphics; third, guidance of the reader into experiences both in and out of school which will broaden his life and extend his mind; and finally, guidance by the teacher which will not only stimulate thinking and involvement but will free the student's mind to function according to his purposes, interests, needs, and level of achievement.

## Classroom Practices

In an attempt to make application of the reading-as-thinking concept to the classroom situation some successful instructional techniques are here presented. The suggestions are by no means intended to be prescriptive. They are offered in the hope that they may stimulate imaginative adaptations on the part of teachers.

### Word Analysis

The advanced student is often interested in the history of words. Resources are available in some of the new basal readers, spellers, and special books devoted to word origins; such as *All Through the*

*Year,* Harper & Row, and *Basic Goals in Spelling,* Webster Division, McGraw-Hill.

Many aids are available for promoting independent word study. Scott, Foresman has a dictionary program which includes six different dictionaries to serve different levels. The series begins with *My Little Pictionary* and advances to a *High School Dictionary.* The latest publications, *In Other Words,* I and II, are thesauruses that explore word meanings, synonyms, antonyms, and words representing sets or collections of things. The able student can work independently with such tools and can develop clarity and precision as he extends his vocabulary.

Harper and Row, Ginn, and Macmillan also have good children's dictionaries.

## Varied Materials

Weekly newspapers such as *My Weekly Reader* and *Scholastic* can become multilevel if a teacher orders a range of levels, such as kindergarten through eighth grade, suited to the range in reading in the classroom. It does not seem wise to order 30 identical copies of a given publication for a given grade level when the reading achievement varies from three grade levels below to three levels above.

Variety in reading materials is needed for the instruction of the advanced reader. Interesting crossword puzzles (Garrard, Continental Press), pictorial encyclopedias (Children's Press), beautifully illustrated books on the several states and regions of America by the same publisher, human interest stories about authors (Walch), the development of folktales from ancient times to the present (Compton's), a series on the childhood of famous American citizens (Bobbs-Merrill), filmstrips on different holidays (Society for Visual Education), and the Newbery and Caldecott selections are representative of the wide selection of materials which should be available for the advanced reader.

## Broadening and Enriching Student Experience

Wide reference reading is valuable for building a background of information. In this regard the following classroom activities might be used:

After a study of Old English, students collected words and listed them. Sentences were then written in which Old English spellings were used: "The yonge Squyer's kyngdom is ferre in the hielands."

Research on different languages was presented in illustrated oral and written reports to the class. Sometimes students combined their efforts:

The Greek alphabet is a branch of Indo-European family of languages. It is related to the Latin and Sanskrit, Slavic, Celtic, and Germanic languages. It is thought to be the most beautiful and effective language ever spoken. Many of our words came from this language.

Commercial materials can enrich listening experiences and strengthen concentration. Programed lessons in listening (Science Research Associates) make a real contribution to the individualization of instruction for the able reader.

## Stimulating Student Involvement

One research project grew out of the reading of a story in a basal text. The story, "Death Trap of the Ages" (*Bright Peaks,* Houghton-Mifflin), presented the springboard for a study of a favorite prehistoric animal. The resource center, family libraries, and the city library provided reading materials. Fossils were brought in. Skills which were involved in the project included locating information, taking notes, comparing resources, and writing reports. The illustrated reports were shared with the class.

Wide reading of good books can be encouraged by providing time for children to share their favorite books. The method chosen should be left to the individual. Possibilities include posters or dioramas that depict a scene from the book, stick-type puppets of favorite characters, book jackets, panel discussions, dramatized scenes, writing a radio script, preparing a book talk, and writing a play based on a favorite book.

Reading poetry can stimulate interest in writing poetry. Many subjects interest children, such as weather, seasons, emotions, and pleasant experiences. Limericks provide another stimulus for writing and for humor.

**Summary**

Reading as thinking depends on the reader's purposes and his repertory of reading skills. Instruction begins with the teacher's evaluation of the reader's functioning skill level, his psychological characteristics, and the nature and quality of his stored information. The advanced reader makes many adjustments in reading approaches as the result of his attention to purpose, the difficulty of material, complexity of theme, and background of knowledge. Variability in rate is the result of the reading-thinking process. The 70s offer new materials and techniques which can be particularly profitable to the advanced reader.

REFERENCES

1. Beery, Althea, Thomas C. Barrett, and William R. Powell (Eds.). *Elementary Reading Instruction*. Boston: Allyn and Bacon, 1969.
2. Schubert, Delwyn G., and Theodore L. Torgerson (Eds.). *Readings in Reading: Practice, Theory, Research*. New York: Thomas Y. Crowell, 1968.
3. Stauffer, Russell G. *Directing Reading as a Cognitive Process*. New York: Harper and Row, 1969.
4. Strang, Ruth, and Dorothy Kendall Bracken. *Making Better Readers*. Boston: D. C. Heath, 1957.

# I'll Never Forget *What's His Name*

Lois V. Arnold
San Diego, California, Public Schools

KEEPING the needs of each student in proper perspective becomes the teacher's challenge for the 70s as increased attention is directed toward Commissioner Allen's mandate of the right to read as a reality for all (*1*). If teachers are to direct attention to the individual to make certain, as Allen has stated, "that no one shall be leaving our schools without the skill and the desire necessary to read to the full limits of his capability," they must sharpen their perception of each student in the context of his experiences, problems, successes, and failures. Thus, education must bring into focus the student who is often overlooked in secondary language arts and reading—the advanced student.

## Who Is He?

In defining the advanced student, Durr's definition of the gifted is applicable in part: The advanced student may be described as the student who is achieving at a high level of academic attainment or who is demonstrating high potential for learning (*7*). Most of the literature points out that the more able students learned to read early in life, probably before they entered school, and have learned to pursue their own interests in reading. As DeBoer states, these students reveal a high correlation between mental abilities and reading comprehension (*5*). However, Robinson notes that they excel because of their intellectual strength, not because of efficiency in study skills (*10*).

These descriptions, which were originally applied to gifted students, apply equally well to the student generally categorized as advanced. In the hypothetical English classroom, the advanced student would be the one who achieves above that level thought of as satisfactory, who is singled out as college bound, and who is able to accomplish most teachers' assignments with a minimum amount of effort.

What are the problems that the advanced student faces in his English class? Smith, Bragstad, and Hesse (13) report a study by Hafter and Douglas, who concluded that thinking skills involved in reading activities are the root of most problems which cause reading difficulties for college students. In this same source, the authors describe a study by Adler in which juniors and seniors in college failed to experience fully the impact of a literary selection because they were reading only superficially.

McCullough (9) points out that when college students experience failure because of reading difficulties, it is not basic skills which are at the root of the trouble but insensitivity to the author's purpose, inability to detect irony, and failure to comprehend difficult words and to interpret allusions and metaphors.

## What Are His Problems?

Recently it was the author's privilege to talk with students in a special independent study program in one of the San Diego high schools. Sitting around a table, the group discussed reading needs of advanced students in high schools and various shortcomings of the reading program. Joe, a serious but articulate student, quietly pointed out that he has great difficulty in reading science and history assignments. He analyzed his own difficulties by saying that his attention wanders and he finds it very difficult to concentrate on the material at hand. Joe has discovered that if he leaves the material for awhile and then rereads it, he may comprehend it. In talking about pleasure reading, such as science fiction, Joe stated that he never has time to read anything in this category.

Nancy, a reserved senior, who kept glancing at her watch as if she regretted every minute spent away from her work, stressed that she has great difficulty in covering all of the material required by honors English. She had taken a course in speed reading, but she felt that this course held no value for her. According to her self-analysis, her major problem was in not knowing how to concentrate and in failing to comprehend what she reads.

Speaking with conviction, Marty maintained that she was aware of the push for speed reading, but she resisted this kind of pressure. She stated that she could read quickly if she wanted to, but she found fast reading to be a very boring activity. Her idea of reading was taking the time to savor what she read as she felt inclined.

When the students suggested improvements for the present reading program, all agreed that, to their knowledge, no emphasis with the exception of speed had been placed upon reading for them since they had been in the sixth grade. They asked for less emphasis on reading for factual information and greater emphasis on reading which would involve thinking and discussing. "Just give us time to read in an exploratory way for enjoyment," implored one.

In addition, members of the group suggested that a program in reading efficiency for them should include greater assistance with reference skills.

These young people also proposed that students be included on book and materials selection committees. Any inclusion of students at present was seen as a token involvement. In pursuing independent study, students found great gaps in available resources in the humanities and would like to share these findings with those responsible for future purchasing of library and curriculum materials.

## What Is the Teacher's Role?

English teachers have a responsibility to consider the process of reading. In their analysis of English instruction today, Squire and Applebee (14) report that only 17 percent of the 95 schools visited offered developmental reading programs. Only seven of the 95 schools had remedial programs in evidence. The conclusion was that the average English teacher does not exert a conscious effort to teach reading as a significant aspect of the English program.

Reading skills receive more attention in most English classes than in any other subject. Teachers emphasize vocabulary required for the study of literature, composition, and language. They stress study skills and word study. As they give students experiences in literature, teachers direct attention to the development of personal tastes and interests as well to the dimension of form and function of literary types.

Although English teachers are expected to act as leaders in

reading programs and although they stress such reading skills, there is evidence that all are not successful. In their report, Squire and Applebee (*14*) suggest that English teachers make little distinction between the teaching of literature for itself and the teaching of students to read literature. A teacher may have his students reading *Julius Caesar* but may fail to make them aware that skills learned in reading this play will help them in the reading of other Shakespearean plays.

Based on what is known of the advanced student and his reading interests and needs, what then does the English teacher do for the seventh grade student? For the ninth grader? For the senior? First of all, the teacher should provide an atmosphere which is completely permeated with reading. The classroom or seminar table should feature books which invite the advanced student to explore, discuss, read, and enjoy. Supplementary materials such as records and films should also be available. Providing an atmosphere of reading is a joint enterprise of the director of the library resource center and the teacher in the English classroom or seminar area.

There must be active interest fostered by the example of the teacher's own reading and by the depth of discussion which occurs. Students must talk about what they read. By merely arousing the student's curiosity, the teacher sparks an interest in the learning process itself.

As the English teacher works with students in assigned and independent reading, he should observe frequently, asking "Are there specific skill difficulties that the advanced student is experiencing?" Here the English teacher must keep informed on specific techniques which can be utilized. Such materials as the *Success in Reading* series (*11*), *Be a Better Reader* series (*12*), and Witty's *How to Improve Your Reading* (*16*) would help teacher and student greatly in knowing what techniques to use to improve rate or increase understanding.

## Who Needs Inservice?

The English teacher who realistically approaches the reading needs of students will appraise his own instructional needs. Perhaps the English department will be the motivating force which kindles an interest on the part of a faculty to help implement an inservice program in reading. Perhaps articulate English teachers, through their professional organizations or in graduate courses, can convince educational planners that teacher training must include not only knowledge of the subject but also understanding of the learning process and of skills needed for that learning. Certainly the teacher who finds himself with little or no knowledge of the books adolescents—including the advanced student—read is not a teacher who can argue the case for a course in literature for adolescents.

If teachers are to help students learn to read critically, and to make assessments of what is heard or viewed or read, the English teacher must learn, as Dale (4) suggests, to ask questions which penetrate, probe, and provoke thought. Recognizing the help that teachers need in making the transition from lecturer-inquisitor to idea-generator and discussion-accelerator, several school systems have provided inservice training for English teachers in the art of questioning.

Assuming that the teacher has accepted his responsibility for teaching critical and creative approaches, how does he make certain that students grow accordingly? When the reading process becomes this kind of thinking process, the teacher is providing experiences in extracting and organizing ideas from material read, in evaluating these ideas, and in reaching conclusions which are valid and logical.

Not enough importance is usually given by teachers to guiding students in deciding on their purpose for reading. As Cramer (3) suggested in a recent article, when the student begins to predict and to set a purpose, he ". . . establishes a dialogue between himself and the author."

As students read novels or short stories, this reading at a higher intellectual level requires educated guesses as to outcomes. Is the writer of fiction skillful in relating cause and effect? Is the author convincing in his development of a character like Ethan Frome, or does he transform a character with a sudden magical twist of a phrase? Can the student detect dialogue which is authentic and that which is contrived? Making predictions requires abilities on the part of students in recognizing the author's purpose and the central theme. Such abilities include that of noting the dexterity with which the author blends description, character portrayal, and dialogue to achieve thematic unity.

How many students have experienced a real dislike for poetry as a result of some well-meaning teacher's analysis of each line, each new word, and each figure of speech? The *Success in Reading* series mentioned earlier includes considerable help for students in developing skills for reading poetry.

Not to be overlooked in the teaching of poetry is the element of pleasure which comes from hearing the music of words or sensing the rhythm of language. There should be the sheer enjoyment of hearing recordings of poets reading their own poetry or of being read to by someone with a true sense of poetic rhythm and with a pleasant voice. Teachers should become acquainted with such delightful collections of poetry as *Reflections on a Gift of Watermelon Pickle* (6) or the series of paperbacks entitled *Voices* (15). Watching students in junior and senior high school pick up such books and turn the pages while looking and reading with interest is evidence in itself that the reading of poetry can be taught if the entry invites and attracts.

## What's His Source?

When reading essays, reviewing articles on topics of specific interest to him, or reacting to editorials from various newspapers or news magazines, the student is faced with making judgments. Who is the writer? What is his background? Where did he obtain his information? When did he write this article? After carefully considering the authority of the writer, the student has information necessary for judging the reliability of the source.

If he is reading biography, is the student aware of the author's viewpoint toward his subject? By knowing the author's qualifications, the student will be able to determine whether the writer is reporting facts or expressing personal biases. Students need the experience of reading opposing points of view, such as differing political philosophies.

In stressing critical reading, the teacher should provide new insights into the interrelatedness of the language arts. The input skills of listening and reading give mutual reinforcement. The hearer or reader must grasp the idea expressed, perceive relationships, and sense emotional overtones. From the output end of communication, the speaker or writer must understand the processes involved in order to effect understanding by his listener or reader. The communicator must realize when there is value in proceeding logically step by step and when to be detached and objective. Many teachers find Altick's *Preface to Critical Reading* (2) of invaluable help for students in both the reading and the writing process. Students are more likely to bring true attitudes of critical inquiry to reading when they themselves have faced the problem of achieving communication that is to be accepted as valid.

## Who Cares?

If dialogue is to be meaningful between the student who has something to say and the teacher who listens, teachers should heed the suggestions given by the students. As an example, in one high school some of the outstanding students felt that they were not having sufficient opportunities to explore contemporary writing in depth. When they asked for a special seminar to be added, there was no time available in their schedules. However, 25 students elected to stay an extra hour after school one day a week to discuss in depth such writers as Flannery O'Connor, William Faulkner, and James Baldwin. The teacher who worked with these students volunteered her services. So much excitement was generated that students throughout the school gathered in informal groups for animated discussions of ideas and philosophies emerging from their reading. Students proposed the books to be read and purchased their own paperbacks or located them in a library. In a follow-up study of these students as they progressed through college, there was a strong indication that this reading in depth had given them critical and creative skills for meeting the college reading tasks.

In another school, advanced students requested help in increasing their reading rate. With no time in their busy schedules for scheduling a reading course, they agreed to attend a reading improvement course at 7:00 A.M. The course concentrated on the importance of knowing the purpose for reading, of learning the organizational arrangement of material, of recognizing stylistic characteristics of an author, and of knowing when to adjust reading rate.

Although the discussion seminar and the reading improvement course were direct results of student requests, other reading programs illustrated the development of approaches as a result of perceptive teachers and administrators who recognize student interests and needs. In several school districts summer reading programs were designed specifically for advanced students. A current trend of providing tutors for students who have serious reading difficulties because of language problems has included utilizing services of more mature students. Although limited in scope, tutorial programs which include advanced students are developing. As the advanced student receives much needed help in becoming sensitive to another's learning problems, valuable side effects may accompany this cooperative approach to learning. Potential leader that he is, the advanced student needs not only to have such sensitivity but also to keep in touch with others by conveying his thoughts styled in language that is understood.

Teachers cannot function effectively without frequent feedback from students. The teacher will want to observe and audit various seminar groups in their discussions of materials read, fiction and nonfiction, and in their reactions to experiences in language and literature. Advanced students will not long feel stilted and inhibited with a teacher present to hear a discussion if they understand the purpose of the auditor. Another procedure is utilizing the tape recorder to record discussion and to encourage students to record their observations and criticisms. Not to be overlooked as a valuable experience is writing done by students, who then develop greater understanding of the speaking voice, be it author or character.

## Focus on You

Advanced students who may lose their identity in English classrooms confront teachers with a real challenge. Perhaps the question is how well the teacher of English can read the signals. In directing his instruction at the "advanced student," is the teacher generalizing 30 or more students into one? Does the teacher provide reading instruction which helps a Joe with his comprehension, a Nancy with her speed, or a Marty with her ability to react creatively? Is the study of *Thanatopsis* an exercise in unlocking word meanings for the sake of understanding a single poem? Or does instruction give students reading techniques which provide entry into the full experience of literature?

Central to the whole process of providing reading instruction for the advanced student in English is a change in strategy. If teachers are to increase the students' effectiveness in reading critically and creatively, teachers must assess their teaching more carefully. The day of rationalizing away results on the basis of the student as the one who fails is past. The challenge of the 70s for the language arts teacher is the student's right to creative instruction in reading.

REFERENCES

1. Allen, James E. "The Right to Read," *Journal of Reading*, 13 (November 1969), 95-101.
2. Altick, Richard D. *Preface to Critical Reading* (5th ed.). New York: Holt, 1960.
3. Cramer, Ronald L. "Setting Purposes and Making Predictions: Essential to Critical Reading," *Journal of Reading*, 13 (January 1970), 259-262.
4. Dale, Edgar. "The Future of Reading," *Reading Teacher*, 23 (December 1969), 205-216.
5. DeBoer, John J. "Creative Reading and the Gifted Student," in William K. Durr (Ed.), *Reading Instruction—Dimensions and Issues*. Houghton Mifflin, 1967, 189-190.
6. Dunning, Stephen, Edward Lueders, and Hugh Smith. *Reflections on a Gift of Watermelon Pickle and Other Modern Verse*. Glenview, Illinois: Scott, Foresman, 1966.
7. Durr, William K. (Ed.). "Reading and the Gifted Student," *Reading Instruction—Dimensions and Issues*. Boston: Houghton Mifflin, 1967, 189-190.
8. Gunn, M. Agnella (Ed.). *What We Know About High School Reading*, a research bulletin prepared by a committee of the National Conference on

Research in English. Champaign, Illinois: National Council of Teachers of English, 1969.

9. McCullough, Constance. "What Does Research Reveal about Practices in Teaching Reading?" in Walter Barbe (Ed.), *Teaching Reading: Selected Materials.* New York: Oxford University Press, 1965, 290-304.

10. Robinson, Francis P. "Study Skills for Superior Students in Secondary Schools," in Laurence E. Hafner (Ed.), *Improving Reading in Secondary Schools.* New York: Macmillan, 1967, 175-180.

11. Shafer, Robert, et al. *Success in Reading, Books 1-6.* Morristown, New Jersey: Silver Burdett, 1968.

12. Smith, Nila Banton. *Be A Better Reader* (3rd ed.). Englewood Cliffs, New Jersey: Prentice Hall, 1969.

13. Smith, Richard J., Bernice Bragstad, and Karl D. Hesse. "Teaching Reading in the Content Areas—An Inservice Model," *Journal of Reading,* 13 (March 1970), 421-428.

14. Squire, James R., and Roger K. Applebee. *High School English Instruction Today.* New York: Appleton-Century-Crofts, 1968.

15. Summerfield, Geoffrey (Ed.). *Voices, Books 1-6.* Chicago: Rand McNally, 1969.

16. Witty, Paul. *How to Improve Your Reading* (revised). Chicago: Science Research Associates, 1963.

# Language Arts for the Academically Talented

HENRY A. BAMMAN
Sacramento State College

THE TRULY CREATIVE is always and precisely that which cannot be taught. And yet, though it seems paradoxical, creativity cannot spring from the untaught. Creativity is the imaginatively gifted recombination of old elements into new. And so, it may be seen that there is no real paradox. The elements of an invention or of a creation cannot be taught; but the creativity must be self-discovered and self-disciplined (*1*).

When we speak of the talented child, whether we view him from a broader point of evidence of his creativity or a rather narrow measure of his intelligence, perhaps we are saying that this child has rather consistently been given opportunities for development that other children have not. Among the many children who are judged to be less talented are those who have, from the very beginning of their school experiences, been denied an opportunity to be creative. As Ciardi states ". . . creativity cannot spring from the untaught." There are probably thousands of children who have come to our schools from meager experience backgrounds. There, because they lacked expressive vocabulary and perhaps were overwhelmed by the models set by teachers and other children, they quietly and unobtrusively withdrew and waited for the recognition which was never given.

Those are the children whose participation in language activities has been sharply curtailed by our perceptions of their capabilities for full involvement. They have become the "remedials," the members of the "slow group," or the "low track." Our methods and our materials, far too often, are narrowed to our perceptions of their inabilities to perform satisfactorily. Who has exposed those children to the beautiful literature, which is their rightful heritage, through the medium of listening, wherein they may gain experiences with good models of language? Who dares to challenge them with

143

telling their own stories? Meager experiences do not necessarily equate with lack of depth of experience. A child with limited experience may have a story to tell if he has a sympathetic audience and someone to record his story for him.

The academically talented child, as he is generally perceived, is one who reads fluently and critically, listens and responds creatively, speaks effectively, commands the attention of his audience, and writes well enough to be understood and to involve his audience in sharing his thoughts. Language is the heart of the individual's intellectual life; and reading, speaking, listening, and writing language are all forms of linguistic usage. We employ the same language, basically, in all forms of our linguistic behavior. When we learn something through one mode, such as listening, we may immediately employ the knowledge gained in writing or reading or speaking. Our comprehension of what we read and hear at any time is limited by our general ability to comprehend. It is general ability to comprehend what one encounters in his environment that differentiates the child of talent from the less able child.

Language itself is creative. Listening to create images intended by the speaker, to recognize stress and intonation as signals of meaning intended by the speaker, and to respond to the speaker's ideas is a creative act. Reading to relate language to symbol, to recognize the meanings of words and sequences of words, to discover the meaning intended by the author, to recognize the writer's intent, and to use what is read for one's own purposes is a creative act. Writing for others—refining and compressing one's thoughts into words and phrases and sentences, with the intention of entertaining, or informing, or convincing a potential reader—is also a creative act. Certainly there is creativity in each spoken message. The speaker begins with a thought to be communicated, calls upon his linguistic storehouse for the right words to express his thoughts, creates recognizable patterns of words, and uses stress and intonation to communicate his ideas. Handwriting and spelling, usually regarded as skill areas which make writing possible, can also be considered to be creative.

Our consideration of creativity in the language arts should not be limited to the child who is fortunate to be academically talented.

Given any language skill, we could demonstrate that its development represents a continuum. At any point on the scale, there is a possibility of aiding a child to be creative as he develops that skill. If we really believe that "creativity is the imaginatively gifted recombination of old elements into new," then whatever level of language a child presents at a given moment can be nurtured toward his more imaginative use of that language. All children, this writer believes, are capable of creative use of language. Some are more capable of self-discovery and self-discipline; they need our assistance, sympathy, and attention as much as the less talented child does. If we assume that children are completely self-directed, they may remain untaught, unstimulated. On the other hand, the child who seems to lack self-discovery and self-discipline needs to know that we regard him as a person who is capable of and worthy of creative participation in all language activities.

What, then, can we do to encourage children to become more creative in the language arts? What opportunities for experiences that may provide insights can we provide in a classroom that will make the difference between the complacent and sometimes bored child and the child who is highly motivated?

*Handwriting.* Handwriting is one of the most highly individualized skills. No two people write exactly alike. Still, we must set standards of form and legibility that will enable the writer to communicate his ideas to another. Good handwriting is a courtesy to the intended reader. The two main goals for the individual are fluency and legibility. Each child will use standard forms as models and, within the limits of his own abilities, develop skill. In the beginning, handwriting is a deeply conscious act; the ultimate goal is for the child to know the forms so well, to have developed coordination to the point of fluency in his writing, that the handwriting itself becomes secondary to expressing one's ideas.

The child should be helped to become critical of his own handwriting skills. He should be worked with individually until he becomes conscious of form, slant, and size of letters. He should be encouraged to write letters to his parents, friends, and relatives. His work can be displayed on the bulletin board and attention called to his accomplishments. The best writers, of both manuscript and cursive styles, can make labels for bulletin boards and other class projects. Many times the child of low intellectual ability will emerge as the star handwriter of the class. He should be recognized and commended for his development of a skill that is basic to written communication.

*Spelling.* When the child must struggle for perfection in handwriting and labors over the spelling of frequently needed words, his chances for expressing himself creatively are seriously hampered. Spelling is a very complex skill. It begins with a thought, and the individual must call upon a visual, auditory, or tactile memory to produce each word. Unfortunately, past instruction in spelling, based on rigidly prescribed word lists for each grade level, has apparently contributed little to the development of children's abilities to spell. Now, with a burst of linguistic knowledge at our fingertips, we view spelling as a skill that has endless possibilities for the individual child. There is no reason that the child who learns to spell the word *walk* should have to wait until another grade level to learn the inflected forms, *walks, walked,* and *walking.* The more able child, whose perceptions are keener than the child of less ability, can be led to see innumerable relationships among words. For instance, when he is confronted with the word *night* in a spelling lesson, he should be led to discover that dozens of words contain the *ight* combination; further, he may be helped to generalize that *i* before *ght* in any word is pronounced with its long sound, a generalization that will help him in pronouncing new words that he encounters in his reading.

To become a really superior speller, the individual must consciously produce cues that will help him generalize from one word to another. It is true that children of low ability benefit little from early introduction in generalizations or/spelling rules. But, the able child can generalize if we aid him in discovering a principle and give him additional examples to which he can apply the generalization. Further, he should be encouraged to find other examples to which the generalization can be applied.

Neither handwriting or spelling skills should take precedence over the expression of ideas. The development of both skills requires repeated practice and application through the need of expressing oneself. It is not sufficient to mark children's errors in spelling and handwriting. We must point out to the children individually *why* the errors were made and help them, through additional practice, to overcome the errors.

*Writing.* All writing is creative. There should be no distinction made, on the basis of creativity, between the child's personal and practical writing. A well-written report is the result of creative endeavor. The child begins with an idea, does sufficient research, organizes his ideas, and finally writes his report. The result should be highly individualistic. When the child creates a poem, he probably has in mind a poetic form which he will attempt to follow. Using his own language, he will attempt to create an expression of feeling or mood and perhaps paint a word picture.

To develop good writers, we must confront them with good literature. They must have frequent experiences with listening to and reading stories and poems and have opportunities to discuss what they have heard and read. The able child can be led to discover the *genre* of literature and to write each type: folktales, fables, historical fiction, biography, and others.

Children should be helped to encapsule their experiences— their fears, their joys, their observations. One group of fourth graders wrote about people's hands, and a little boy whom we had perceived as a child of low ability wrote, "The priest's hands are soft and white like a pillow. I think he uses his hands to touch God."

Children of all levels of ability can write group stories. The able scribe records the expressions of the child who finds writing and spelling difficult. Matters of style and punctuation can be discussed and decided cooperatively. One approach which can be used is to confront six different groups of children with the same picture or experience and separate them during their writing. Subsequent reading of their stories should yield an excellent example of how well they can create from their own ideas.

*Oral expression.* Storytelling provides a transition from passive enjoyment to creative participation. When a child tells a story, he has many opportunities for expressing his own creativity. He may elaborate through the use of his own words; he may use stress, intonation, and gestures to communicate his story. There is no greater compliment than the honest response of peers to a story well told.

A good storyteller must know his story well, study his story carefully to determine the need for gestures and facial expressions, attempt to represent his characters faithfully, and use voice qualities that are appropriate for the story. Good storytellers can share their talents with younger children or with groups of children in their own class who are too timid to participate.

Puppets, shadowboxes, and flannel boards are appropriate vehicles for some storytelling activities. Artistic children can be encouraged to make their own puppets; it is amazing how a timid child frequently gains confidence when he tells his story through a paper and cloth medium.

Oral reading and storytelling are valuable not only as a means of a child's developing his own expression but also as a means of developing listening skills. As children listen to oral presentations of their peers or their teacher, they gain added feeling for and knowledge of the many patterns of language which they themselves may be encouraged to use.

*Reading.* Of prime concern to all of us should be a child's development of reading skills and interests that will sustain him for the rest of his life. In our concern for teaching the child how to read, we frequently kill the desire to continue reading after he leaves school. Reading, like all of the language arts, encompasses skills, attitudes, and interests. It was Thoreau who said that "most men read to satisfy a paltry convenience." The writer fears that too much of our instruction in reading fails to awaken in the child a desire to use reading for satisfaction of his needs for information, for conviction, and for pleasure.

If a child is to become a creative reader, he must be surrounded by good books of all types and of a variety of levels of difficulty. When we discover, through a selection in the basal reader which is used to aid a child in developing skills, that there is high interest in a particular selection, we should rise to the challenge. Books should be provided to extend beyond that selection and lead the child to discover that for every idea developed in a particular selection there are dozens of selections that treat the idea in other settings, through our characters, or through additional but related ideas. We are developing good readers only if we have evidence that each child is applying his skills to ever increasing levels of difficulty and maturity of ideas.

We have evidence of creative reading in the classroom when we observe children seeking a variety of sources to extend their knowledge and using that knowledge to communicate better with their classmates. We have evidence of creativity when a child seizes a book and reads it from cover to cover, impatient to share it with others or find another which will deepen his convictions. We have evidence of creativity when a child weeps unashamedly or laughs heartily with a character that he has discovered in a story.

When children adapt the plot of a story or an incident and dramatize it for their classmates, when a child yearns to read aloud a poem or a story to his friends, or when reading or listening to a story or poem leads a child to write his own story or poem, we have evidence of creative activity. As we observe our children assimilate words and make them a part of their oral and written expression, when we hear a child drop his dialect and employ a more formal expression of language because it is appropriate for the occasion, or when we observe that a child's patterns of language have slowly and painfully developed to more complex patterns, we have evidence that there has been creative growth. Best of all, when we as teachers observe that a child has modified his behavior and has become more critical of himself, more self-directed in his speaking, listening, writing, and reading, and more aware of the possibilities of using his language arts to create a world in which he functions better as an individual, we have unquestionable evidence that something worthwhile has been created.

REFERENCE

1. Ciardi, John. *Saturday Review,* December 15, 1956.